LIVING IN JAPAN

PHOTOS RETO GUNTLI / TEXT ALEX KERR / KATHY ARLYN SOKOL

LIVING IN JAPAN

EDITED BY / HERAUSGEGEBEN VON / SOUS LA DIRECTION DE

ANGELIKA TASCHEN

TASCHEN

KÖLN LONDON LOS ANGELES MADRID PARIS TOKYO

Japan Sea

TOTTORI

OKAYAMA   KYOTO

SHIMANE   HIROSHIMA   HYOGO   • Ky

Akashi • • Kobe
• Osaka

YAMAGUCHI   • Hiroshima   • Naoshima   NA

I n l a n d   S e a   • Mure
KAGAWA

TOKUSHIMA   WAKAYAMA

SAGA   EHIME   • Iya

FUKUOKA   SHIKOKU ISLAND   KOCHI

NAGASAKI

OITA

• Nagasaki

KUMAMOTO

MIYAZAKI

Contents / Inhalt / Sommaire

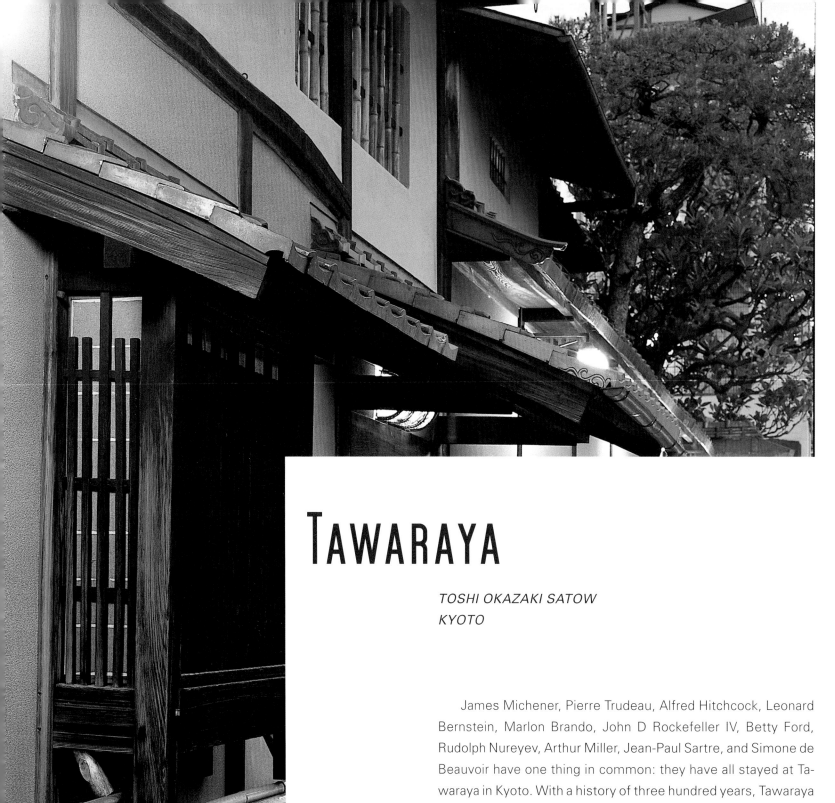

Tawaraya

TOSHI OKAZAKI SATOW
KYOTO

James Michener, Pierre Trudeau, Alfred Hitchcock, Leonard Bernstein, Marlon Brando, John D Rockefeller IV, Betty Ford, Rudolph Nureyev, Arthur Miller, Jean-Paul Sartre, and Simone de Beauvoir have one thing in common: they have all stayed at Tawaraya in Kyoto. With a history of three hundred years, Tawaraya is the queen of Japan's traditional *ryokan* (inns). Toshi Okazaki Satow, the 11th-generation owner, maintains Tawaraya's tradition of reserve and cultural nuance, providing a carefully controlled balance between modern comforts, and scrolls, lacquered furniture, and flower arrangements. Tawaraya's street entrance is so small one could walk right past it without noticing; there is no lobby, just a small reading room, and some nooks to sit and relax; corridors with flowers; and the rooms, all looking out on a private corner of a perfectly tended garden. Each room is a refuge; the garden, the tables and chairs are designed with attention to every detail. It's the tradition of tea ceremony and classic hospitality compressed into just eighteen rooms in the heart of busy modern Kyoto.

Leaning bamboo racks, used to protect the lower parts of walls from dirt or damage, rest against the façade of the 18th-century inn.

Bambusgestelle, die den unteren Wandbereich vor Schmutz und Beschädigungen schützen sollen, lehnen an der Fassade dieses Gästehauses aus dem 18. Jahrhundert.

Appuyées contre la façade de cette auberge du 18ᵉ siècle, des structures en bambou protègent le bas des murs de la boue et des coups.

James Michener, Pierre Trudeau, Alfred Hitchcock, Leonard Bernstein, Marlon Brando, John D. Rockefeller IV., Betty Ford, Rudolf Nurejew, Arthur Miller, Jean-Paul Sartre und Simone de Beauvoir haben eines gemeinsam: Sie alle haben im Tawaraya in Kyoto übernachtet. Tawaraya, das auf eine dreihundertjährige Geschichte zurückblicken kann, ist das Nonplusultra unter Japans traditionellen Gästehäusern oder *ryokan*. Toshi Okazaki Satow, Eigentümer in der 11. Generation, bewahrt die Tradition des Tawaraya als kulturellen Rückzugsort und sorgt für ein ausgewogenes Gleichgewicht zwischen modernem Komfort, Schriftrollen, Lackmöbeln und Blumenarrangements. Der Straßeneingang des Tawaraya ist so klein, dass man ihn leicht übersieht. Es gibt keine Lobby, nur ein kleines Lesezimmer und ein paar ruhige Sitze. Die Flure sind blumengeschmückt und die Zimmer gehen alle auf einen eigenen, perfekt gepflegten Gartenanteil hinaus. Jedes der gerade einmal 18 Zimmer bildet einen Rückzugsort, an dem der Gast die klassische japanische Gastlichkeit im modernen Japan findet.

James Michener, Pierre Trudeau, Alfred Hitchcock, Leonard Bernstein, Marlon Brando, John D. Rockefeller IV, Betty Ford, Rudolph Noureyev, Arthur Miller, Jean-Paul Sartre et Simone de Beauvoir ont tous en commun d'avoir séjourné à la Tawaraya de Kyoto. Avec ses trois siècles d'histoire, Tawaraya est la perle des *ryokan* (auberges) traditionnelles. Elle appartient depuis onze générations à la famille de l'actuel propriétaire, Toshi Okazaki Satow, qui veille sur sa tradition de retenue et de subtilité culturelle, offrant un équilibre savant entre le confort moderne, les rouleaux, les meubles laqués et les arrangements floraux. L'entrée principale est si petite qu'on passe facilement devant sans la voir. Il n'y a pas de hall, juste une salle de lecture et des recoins où s'asseoir et se détendre. Les couloirs fleuris et les chambres donnent tous sur un petit coin privatif du jardin parfaitement entretenu. Chaque pièce est un refuge avec un grand raffinement du détail. Les traditions d'hospitalité et de la cérémonie du thé ont été condensées dans ces dix-huit chambres en plein cœur de la ville moderne et animée.

10

LEFT ABOVE:
A bamboo ladle sits atop a moss-laden stone purification basin laid in a pebble-strewn bed.

LEFT BELOW:
A slanting beam of light against the earth-tempered walls illuminates a woven straw rain hat.

RIGHT:
A stone lantern (ishi-doro), originally found in the gardens of temples and shrines, complements the tamba-ware pot in the foreground.

LINKS OBEN:
Eine Bambusschöpfkelle ruht auf einem bemoosten Reinigungsbecken aus Naturstein, das von einem Kiesbett umgeben ist.

LINKS UNTEN:
Ein schräg einfallender Lichtstrahl beleuchtet einen geflochtenen Strohhut an der lehmfarbenen Wand.

RECHTE SEITE:
Eine Steinlaterne (ishi-doro), wie sie es ursprünglich nur in Tempel- und Schreingärten gab, bildet eine schöne Ergänzung zum Tamba-Steingutkrug im Vordergrund.

EN HAUT, À GAUCHE, :
Une louche en bambou sur un bassin de purification en pierre envahi de mousse au milieu d'un lit de galets.

EN BAS, À GAUCHE:
Un faisceau de lumière oblique sur le mur couleur terre illumine un chapeau de pluie en paille.

PAGE DE DROITE:
Une lanterne en pierre (ishi-doro), comme on en trouvait dans les jardins des temples et sanctuaires, complète le pot en tamba au premier plan.

TAWARAYA / KYOTO

Iori Nishioshikoji-cho

KYOTO

Kyoto's city center once boasted thousands of *machiya* "townhouses," but during the latter half of the 20th century, most of these were torn down. In 2004, Alex Kerr and associates established Iori for the purpose of acquiring threatened *machiya*, restoring them, and offering them as places where visitors can experience traditional arts and Kyoto living. One of Iori's *machiya* is Nishioshikoji-cho. Constructed ca. 1890, the house is a large-scale structure, restored in pure Japanese style. It displays typical features of townhouse architecture, such as the rough-hewn beams on the ceiling of the top floor, interior gardens (*tsuboniwa*, or "gardens in a bottle"), and *mushiko-mado* plaster slits letting in light from the street at the upper level. Decorations include round *andon* floor lamps, bamboo baskets with flower arrangements, *sudare* hangings made of split bamboo, and Edo period *byobu* folding screens. Resonant with images of Chinese landscapes and poetry, they bring into the house a feeling of the classical culture of which Kyoto was for centuries the center.

Das Zentrum Kyotos konnte einst mit tausenden von Stadthäusern (machiya) aufwarten, doch in der zweiten Hälfte des 20. Jahrhunderts wurden die meisten davon abgerissen. Im Jahr 2004 gründeten Alex Kerr und seine Geschäftspartner Iori, mit dem Ziel, bedrohte machiya aufzukaufen, sie zu restaurieren und an Besucher zu vermieten, die die traditionellen Künste und das Leben in Kyoto kennen lernen wollen. Eines dieser Iori machiya ist das Nishioshikoji-cho. Das um 1890 in der späten Edo-Zeit errichtete, groß angelegte Gebäude wurde im japanischen Stil restauriert. Es weist typische Merkmale der Stadthaus-Architektur auf wie die grob behauenen Deckenbalken des obersten Stockwerks, kleine Innengärten (tsuboniwa) und Fensterschlitze im Obergeschoss (mushiko-mado), die Licht von der Straße hereinlassen. Zu den dekorativen Einrichtungsgegenständen zählen runde Laternen (andon), Bambuskörbe mit Blumenarrangements, Bambusrollos (sudare) sowie Stellschirme (byobu) aus der Edo-Zeit. Letztere sind mit chinesischen Tuschelandschaften und Gedichten verziert und verleihen dem Haus eine klassische Kultur.

Le cœur de Kyoto comptait autrefois des milliers de machiya (maisons de ville) dont la plupart ont été détruites dans la seconde moitié du 20e siècle. En 2004, Alex Kerr et ses associés ont fondé la société Iori afin de racheter ces demeures en danger, les restaurer et les reconvertir en lieux où les visiteurs pourraient goûter à l'art de vivre et aux arts traditionnels de Kyoto. Nishioshikoji-cho en est une. Construite vers 1890, c'est une vaste bâtisse restaurée dans le pur style japonais. Elle présente les caractéristiques typiques de la machiya, tels que les poutres apparentes en bois brut du dernier étage, les tsuboniwa intérieurs (ou « jardins en bouteille ») et, à l'étage, les mushiko-mado (meurtrières en plâtre) qui laissent filtrer la lumière de la rue. La décoration inclut des andon (lampadaires ronds), des paniers en bambou contenant des arrangements floraux, des sudare (stores) en éclats de bambou et des paravents byobu de la période Edo. Évoquant les paysages et la poésie chinoises, ces derniers ajoutent encore à l'atmosphère de culture classique dont Kyoto fut le centre pendant des siècles.

Yukimi-shoji (papered
sliding doors with a glass
cut-out), and a marumado
(circular window) with
patterned latticework,
frame the view across
rooms and gardens.

Yukimi-shoji (papierbe-
spannte Schiebetüren mit
einer Glasaussparung)
sowie ein marumado
(Rundfenster) mit Holzgitter rahmen den Blick auf
Zimmer und Gärten.

Des yukimi-shoji (portes
coulissantes percées
d'une vitre) et un maru-
mado (fenêtre ronde) orné
d'un treillis encadrent
la vue sur l'enfilade de
pièces et de jardins.

14

LEFT ABOVE:
Powerful wooden beams support the ceiling of the tatami-matted top-floor room. Solid-paneled closet doors reflect light from the windows.

LEFT BELOW:
A marumado (circular window) with a view of the garden. The plaster has been cut away to reveal the wall's internal structure of crisscross bamboo.

RIGHT ABOVE:
A single peony blossom, set in a woven bamboo basket, speaks of spring.

RIGHT BELOW:
A steep traditional Kyoto staircase descends to the wood-floored entryway.

FOLLOWING DOUBLE PAGE:
Bedding, a book, a table with incense burner, a flower vase, and a cup of tea – in front of an Edo period folding screen with a painting of sages in a mountain hermitage.

LINKE SEITE OBEN:
Mächtige Holzbalken stützen die Decke des tatami-Zimmers im Obergeschoss. Solide vertäfelte Schranktüren reflektieren das einfallende Licht.

LINKE SEITE UNTEN:
Ein marumado (Rundfenster) mit Blick in den Garten. Der Gipsputz wurde weggeschlagen, um die Bambusgitterstruktur sichtbar zu machen.

RECHTS OBEN:
Eine einzelne Pfingstrosenblüte in einem geflochtenen Bambuskorb kündigt den Frühling an.

RECHTS UNTEN:
Die steile, traditionelle Treppe im Kyoto-Stil führt in den mit Holzdielen ausgelegten Eingangsbereich.

FOLGENDE DOPPELSEITE:
Schlaflager, Buch, Tisch mit Räuchergefäß, Blumenvase und eine Tasse Tee vor einem Stellschirm aus der Edo-Zeit, der Gelehrte vor einer Bergklause zeigt.

PAGE DE GAUCHE, EN HAUT:
De solides poutres soutiennent le plafond de la chambre à l'étage au sol recouvert de tatamis. Les portes de placard en bois verni reflètent la lumière du jour.

PAGE DE GAUCHE, EN BAS:
Le jardin vu au travers d'un marumado (fenêtre ronde). Le plâtre a été gratté pour révéler la structure interne du mur en entrecroisement de bambous.

À DROITE, EN HAUT:
Une pivoine dans un panier en bambou évoque le printemps.

À DROITE, EN BAS:
La pente raide d'un escalier traditionnel de Kyoto donnant sur l'entrée parquetée.

DOUBLE PAGE SUIVANTE:
Un lit, un livre, une table avec un brûleur d'encens, un vase et une tasse de thé, devant un paravent de l'époque Edo représentant des sages dans un ermitage de montagne.

IORI NISHIOSHIKOJI-CHO / KYOTO

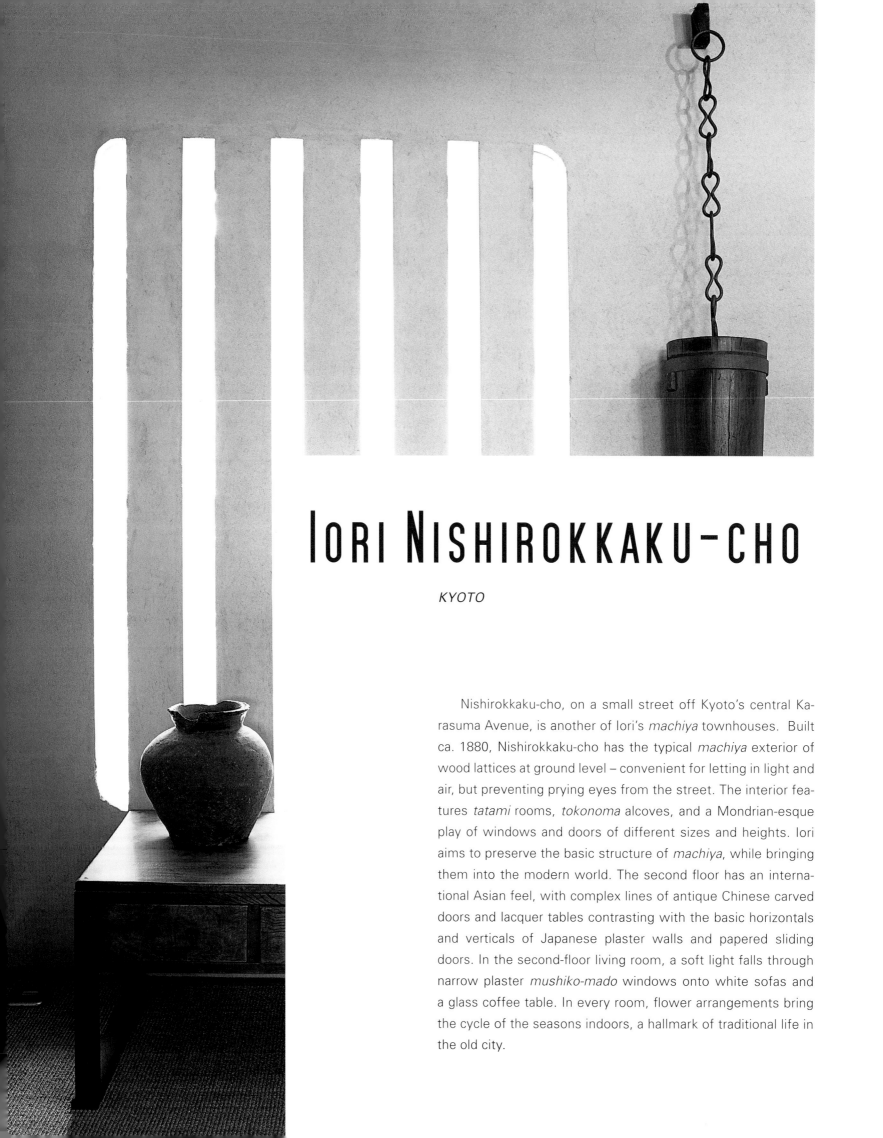

Iori Nishirokkaku-cho

KYOTO

Nishirokkaku-cho, on a small street off Kyoto's central Karasuma Avenue, is another of Iori's *machiya* townhouses. Built ca. 1880, Nishirokkaku-cho has the typical *machiya* exterior of wood lattices at ground level – convenient for letting in light and air, but preventing prying eyes from the street. The interior features *tatami* rooms, *tokonoma* alcoves, and a Mondrian-esque play of windows and doors of different sizes and heights. Iori aims to preserve the basic structure of *machiya*, while bringing them into the modern world. The second floor has an international Asian feel, with complex lines of antique Chinese carved doors and lacquer tables contrasting with the basic horizontals and verticals of Japanese plaster walls and papered sliding doors. In the second-floor living room, a soft light falls through narrow plaster *mushiko-mado* windows onto white sofas and a glass coffee table. In every room, flower arrangements bring the cycle of the seasons indoors, a hallmark of traditional life in the old city.

A deep cedar tub. The bucket and paneled walls are also cedar. The window looks out into the garden.

Ein tiefer Badezuber aus Zedernholz. Eimer und Wandvertäfelung sind ebenfalls aus Zedernholz. Das Fenster geht auf den Garten hinaus.

Une profonde baignoire en cèdre. Le seau et les boiseries sont également en cèdre. La fenêtre donne sur le jardin.

Ein weiteres von Ioris Stadthäusern *(machiya)* ist das Nishirokkaku-cho, das in einer kleinen Seitenstraße der großen Karasuma Avenue von Kyoto liegt. Das um 1880 errichtete Haus weist im Erdgeschoss eine typische *machiya*-Fassade in Holzlattenbauweise auf – sie lässt Licht und Luft herein, schützt aber gleichzeitig vor neugierigen Blicken. In seinem Inneren gibt es *tatami*-Zimmer, *tokonoma* (Alkoven) und ein an Mondrian-Bilder erinnerndes Spiel von Fenster und Türen. Die Iori-Foundation bemüht sich, die Originalbauweise der *machiya* zu erhalten, sie aber gleichzeitig ins Hier und Heute zu holen. Der erste Stock atmet ein international-asiatisches Flair. Reich verzierte Türen und Lacktische kontrastieren mit den nüchternen Horizontalen und Vertikalen japanischer Ziegelwände und papierner Schiebetüren. Im Wohnzimmer fällt gedämpftes Licht durch die schmalen Fens-terschlitze *(mushiko-mado)* und bringt weiße Sofas und einen gläsernen Couchtisch zum Strahlen. In jedem Zimmer repräsentieren Blumenarrangements die jeweiligen Jahreszeiten – ein typisches Merkmal für das traditionelle Leben in der Altstadt.

Située dans une ruelle donnant sur l'avenue centrale Karasuma, Nishirokkaku-cho est une autre de ces *machiya*. Construite vers 1880, elle présente une façade typique avec un treillage en bois au rez-de-chaussée, qui laisse filtrer l'air et la lumière tout en préservant l'intimité. Les pièces aux sols recouverts de *tatamis* comportent des *tokonoma* (alcôves). Les fenêtres et les portes de tailles et de hauteurs différentes créent un effet à la Mondrian. Iori conserve la structure de base de la *machiya* tout en la projetant dans la modernité. L'étage est typique du style international asiatique, avec d'anciennes portes sculptées chinoises et des tables laquées qui contrastent avec les lignes horizontales et verticales des murs en plâtre et des portes en papier coulissantes. Dans le salon, les *mushiko-mado* (meurtrières) diffusent une lumière douce sur les canapés blancs et la table basse en verre. Dans chaque chambre, des arrangements floraux reproduisent le cycle des saisons, dans la pure tradition de la vieille cité.

LEFT ABOVE:
Wild iris in a narrow-necked bronze jar stands in front of latticed paper shoji windows.

LEFT BELOW:
Purple iris in a narrow-necked blue and white ceramic jar stand beside plaster slatted mushiko-mado window.

RIGHT ABOVE:
At night, light from within spills out through wooden lattices at street level and plaster mushiko-mado windows on the second floor.

RIGHT BELOW:
White plaster walls, admit light through vertical slatted mushiko-mado windows onto white sofas, a contrast of old and new.

LINKS OBEN:
Eine wilde Schwertlilie in einer schmalen hohen Bronzevase steht vor einem papierbespannten Schiebefenster (shoji).

LINKS UNTEN:
Eine lilafarbene Schwertlilie in einem schlanken blauweißen Keramikgefäß neben Fensterschlitzen im Mauerwerk (mushiko-mado).

RECHTE SEITE OBEN:
Nachts dringt Licht durch die Holzgitter im Erdgeschoss sowie durch die Fensterschlitze (mushiko-mado) im ersten Stock.

RECHTE SEITE UNTEN:
Weiß verputzte, vertikale Fensterschlitze (mushiko-mado) lassen Licht auf die weißen Sofas fallen: Ein schöner Kontrast zwischen Alt und Neu.

EN HAUT, À GAUCHE:
Un iris sauvage dans un vase en bronze au col étroit devant une fenêtre shoji treillissée en papier.

EN BAS, À GAUCHE:
Un iris mauve dans un vase en céramique bleue et blanche au col étroit, près de meurtrières en plâtre mushiko-mado.

PAGE DE DROITE, EN HAUT:
La nuit, la lumière de la maison filtre entre les lattes en bois au niveau de la rue et hors des mushiko-mado en plâtre à l'étage.

PAGE DE DROITE, EN BAS:
La lumière filtrant entre les fentes verticales des mushiko-mado illumine les murs en plâtre et les canapés blancs, soulignant le contraste entre l'ancien et le moderne.

22

IORI NISHIROKKAKU-CHO / KYOTO

LEFT PAGE:
An arrangement of clematis set in a bamboo vase in the form of a water bucket, illuminated by light from the garden.

RIGHT PAGE:
View of the upstairs bedroom with tatami mats and a wood-floored tokonoma alcove, with a framed ink drawing, table with flowers, and small paper shoin windows.

LINKE SEITE:
Licht aus dem Garten fällt auf eine Clematis, die in einer eimerförmigen Bambusvase arrangiert wurde.

RECHTE SEITE:
Ein Blick in das Schlafzimmer im Obergeschoss mit Binsenmatten (tatami), einer mit Holzdielen ausgelegten Nische (tokonoma), die eine gerahmte Tuschzeichnung sowie einen blumengeschmückten Tisch enthält. Das Schlafzimmer verfügt über kleine papierbespannte shoin-Fenster.

PAGE DE GAUCHE:
Une clématite dans un vase en bambou en forme de seau, éclairée par la lumière provenant du jardin.

24

PAGE DE DROITE:
Vue d'angle de la chambre à l'étage, avec des tatamis, une alcôve tokonoma parquetée, une encre de Chine encadrée, une fleur sur une table basse et des petites fenêtres shoin en papier.

In the upstairs bedroom, delicate wood strips on the paper yukimi-shoji doors, the lower section made of glass, contrast with the strong lattice-work of antique Chinese panels.

FOLLOWING PAGE LEFT:
Detail from an Edo period (1603-1868) folding screen, of a white heron on a albizia branch.

FOLLOWING PAGE RIGHT:
Guest bedding lies in front of the tokonoma alcove, with grasses and wild-flowers in a bamboo vase, lit by light from the garden flowing through the low shoin window.

Im Schlafzimmer bilden die zierlichen Holzlatten der papierbespannten Schiebetüren mit Glas-aussparung (yukimi-shoji) einen schönen Kontrast zu dem Gitterwerk antiker chinesischer Stellschirme.

FOLGENDE SEITE LINKS:
Detail eines Stellschirms aus der Edo-Zeit (1603–1868). Es zeigt einen weißen Reiher auf einem Seidenbaumzweig.

FOLGENDE SEITE RECHTS:
Das Gästeschlaflager be-findet sich direkt vor der traditionellen Ziernische (tokonoma) mit Gräsern und Wildblumen in einer Bambusvase. Aus dem Garten fällt durch das beinahe bis zum Boden reichende shoin-Fenster direkt Licht auf die Nische.

Dans la chambre, les délicats montants en bois des portes en papier yuki-mi-shoji, dont la partie in-férieure est en verre, con-trastent avec le robuste treillage des anciennes boiseries chinoises.

PAGE SUIVANTE, A GAUCHE:
Détail d'un paravent de la période Edo (1603-1868), représentant un héron blanc sur une branche d´albizia.

PAGE SUIVANTE, A DROITE:
Le lit d'amis devant l'alcôve tokonoma, avec des herbes et des fleurs sauvages dans un vase en bambou, baigné par la lumière du jardin à travers une fenêtre basse shoin.

26

Sugimoto House

UTAKO SUGIMOTO
KYOTO

Of surviving Kyoto *machiya*, the Sugimoto House is the largest and most beautifully maintained. Rich in the appurtenances of Kyoto merchant wealth – folding screens, *fusuma* (padded paper doors) in winter, bamboo doors in summer, a gold-lacquered Buddhist altar – this is the last of the mansions where the full flavor of life in the old city can still be tasted. Founded by a kimono wholesaler in 1767, the present structure dates from 1870. The street frontage, half a block long, features Kyoto-style lattice work, a bay window, *inuyarai* (bamboo slats protecting the lower wall), *mushiko-mado* plaster slatted windows, and tiled roofs of different levels. Inside, the house reveals itself in a series of shifting views: a garden glimpsed through a corridor, the mats of the *zashiki* (sitting room) seeming to flow through *sudare* blinds hung in receding perspective. The complex is massive, with an eight-meter-high open kitchen and three *kura* storehouses walled with thick plaster, but the interior effect is of delicacy. A single floor lamp, a lantern, and a candle can be seen.

Reflected in the glass of a yukimi-shoji door, a round andon floor lamp stands in front of orange fusuma (paper doors) stenciled with crests in mica.

In der Glasaussparung einer papierbespannten Schiebetür (yukimi-shoji) spiegelt sich eine runde Stehlampe (andon). Sie steht vor einer orangefarbenen Papiertür (fusuma), die mit glitzernden Wappen geschmückt ist.

Se reflétant dans la vitre d'une porte yukimi-shoji, un lampadaire andon rond devant un fusuma (porte en papier) orange peint au pochoir de motifs micas.

Von den erhaltenen *machiya* in Kyoto ist das Sugimoto House das größte und besterhaltene. Angefüllt mit Reichtümern von Kyotos wohlhabenden Kaufleuten wie Stellschirmen, *fusuma* (Schiebetüren) im Winter bzw. Bambustüren im Sommer und einem goldlackierten Altar, ist es das letzte Stadthaus, in dem man das Leben der alten Stadt heute noch spüren kann. Erbaut wurde das Haus 1767 von einem Kimonogroßhändler, die heutige Bausubstanz geht allerdings auf das Jahr 1870 zurück. Die Straßenfront, die einen halben Block lang ist, ist in der Kyoto-typischen Lattenbauweise gehalten. Es gibt ein Erkerfenster, *inuyarai* (Bambusleisten, die die unteren Wände schützen), *mushiko-mado* (Fensterschlitze) und Ziegeldächer auf verschiedenen Ebenen. In seinem Inneren bietet das Haus eine Reihe verschiedener Perspektiven: ein Gang gewährt Ausblick auf den Garten, die *tatami*-Matten des *zashiki* (Salon) bilden eine Einheit mit den perspektivisch zurücktretenden Rollos *(sudare)*. Das riesige Gebäude verfügt über eine acht Meter hohe offene Küche und drei *kura* (Lagerhäuser).

De toutes les *machiya* à avoir survécu, Sugimoto est la plus vaste et la plus superbement entretenue. Avec ses paravents, ses *fusuma* (portes matelassées en papier) l'hiver, ses portes en bambou l'été, son autel bouddhiste laquée en or, elle reflète l'opulence des riches marchands de Kyoto d'autrefois et l'on peut encore y goûter à l'art de vivre de la vieille cité. La maison fut construite en 1767 par un grossiste en kimonos mais la partie visible aujourd'hui date de 1870. La façade, qui fait la moitié d'un pâté de maisons, est en treillage de Kyoto, avec un bow-window, un *inuyarai* (plinthe en lattes de bambou), des *mushiko-mado* (meurtrières en plâtre) et des toits en tuiles de hauteurs différentes. À l'intérieur, le regard se perd dans un jeu de perspectives : un jardin entraperçu au bout d'un couloir, les tapis du *zashiki* (salon) semblant flotter au travers de *sudare* (stores) suspendus en arrière-plan. Le complexe massif a une cuisine ouverte de huit mètres sous plafond et trois entrepôts *kur*. Pourtant, il règne une atmosphère délicate : on remarque ici et là un lampadaire isolé, une lanterne, une bougie.

LEFT ABOVE:
The skylit genkan, or entryway, has two entrances: to the right, for daily use, leading to the kitchen; and to the left, for visitors, leading to the house proper.

LEFT BELOW:
A trivet supports an iron kettle (tetsubin) for making green tea in the wooden brazier (hako-hibachi). To the left is a basket of charcoal for the tea ceremony.

RIGHT ABOVE:
Room arranged for summer, with hanging misu blinds. These exceptionally luxurious misu, with graduated patterns of split bamboo, are trimmed with blue and white wave patterns.

RIGHT BELOW:
The ornate Buddhist altar suggests the wealth and taste of old Kyoto merchant families. It displays the finest craft in wood carving, lacquer, gold, and metal fittings.

FOLLOWING DOUBLE PAGE:
The verdant garden contains in a small space the classic ingredientrs: brush and bamboo fences, a purification basin with ladle, a mossy stone lantern, and decorative stones.

LINKE SEITE OBEN:
Von dem mit Oberlichtern versehenen genkan oder Eingangsbereich gehen zwei Türen ab: die rechte dient dem täglichen Gebrauch und führt in die Küche, während die linke Besuchern vorbehalten ist und in die eigentlichen Wohnräume führt.

LINKE SEITE UNTEN:
Ein Dreifuß trägt einen gusseisernen Kessel (tetsubin), in dem auf dem hölzernen Kohlebecken (hako-hibachi) grüner Tee zubereitet wird. Links davon steht ein Korb mit Holzkohle für die Teezeremonie.

RECHTS OBEN:
Dieser Raum wurde mit Jalousien (misu) für den Sommer eingerichtet. Die außergewöhnlich edlen misu mit ihren verschiedenen Mustern aus gespaltenem Bambus werden von weißblauen Wellenmustern eingefasst.

RECHTS UNTEN:
Der geschmückte buddhistische Altar spiegelt den Wohlstand und Geschmack der alten Kyotoer Kaufmannsfamilien wieder. Die Kunsthandwerker, die ihn schufen, waren Meister im Holzschnitzen, Lackieren und Anfertigen von Gold- und Metalleinlegearbeiten.

FOLGENDE DOPPELSEITE:
Dieser grüne Garten vereint auf engstem Raum alles, was zu einem klassischen japanischen Garten gehört: Reisig- und Bambuszäune, ein Reinigungsbecken samt Schöpfkelle, eine bemooste Steinlaterne und dekorative Natursteine.

PAGE DE GAUCHE, EN HAUT:
Éclairé par une verrière, le genkan (vestibule) possède deux entrées: celle de droite, pour tous les jours, mène à la cuisine ; celle de gauche, pour les visiteurs, à la maison proprement dite.

PAGE DE GAUCHE, EN BAS:
Dans un brasero en bois (hako-hibachi) un trépied soutient une bouilloire en fonte (tetsubin) pour préparer le thé vert. À gauche, un panier de charbon de bois pour la cérémonie du thé.

EN HAUT, À DROITE:
Le décor d'été avec des stores misu. Exceptionnellement luxueux, ces derniers sont ornés de motifs nuancés en éclats de bambou et bordés de vagues bleues et blanches.

EN BAS, À DROITE:
L'autel bouddhiste, superbement ouvragé en bois sculpté, laque, or et incrustations de métal, témoigne de la richesse et du goût des vieilles familles marchandes de Kyoto.

DOUBLE PAGE SUIVANTE:
Dans un espace réduit, le jardin verdoyant contient tous les ingrédients classiques : une palissade en jonc et bambou, un bassin de purification avec sa louche, une lanterne en pierre couverte de mousse et des pierres d'ornement.

SUGIMOTO HOUSE / KYOTO

YOSHIDA SANSO

KYOKO NAKAMURA
KYOTO

After the capital moved to Tokyo in 1868, followed by the disestablishment of the nobility in 1945, most of Kyoto's princely estates disappeared. One of the few remaining is Yoshida Sanso, originally built for Prince Higashi-Fushimi, the brother-in-law of the Showa Emperor (Hirohito) in 1932. Run as a *ryokan* (traditional inn) and restaurant since 1948, Yoshida Sanso stands in northeast Kyoto in an area surrounded by old shrines and temples. Carpenters used the finest *hinoki* cedar from the Kiso region to build it. With a wide garden, high gate, and curving driveway, the feeling is expansive, with a delicate rise to the eaves of the copper roofs. Reflecting modish style of the 30is, Yoshida Sanso incorporates art deco touches such as the chandelier and stained-glass windows in the vestibule and upstairs rooms. The proprietor Kyoko Nakamura is a calligrapher, and her brushwork features in signs and menus. While keeping the mansion in its original form, the Nakamuras use carefully chosen objects (flowers, candle-sticks, tables, trays, dishes) to create an air of princely grace.

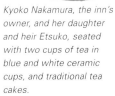

Kyoko Nakamura, the inn's owner, and her daughter and heir Etsuko, seated with two cups of tea in blue and white ceramic cups, and traditional tea cakes.

Kyoko Nakamura, die Eigentümerin des Gäste-hauses, und ihre Tochter und Nachfolgerin Etsuko mit zwei Tassen Tee aus blauweißer Keramik und traditionellen Teeküchlein.

Kyoko Nakamura, la propriétaire de l'auberge, avec sa fille et héritiè-re Etsuko, devant deux tasses en céramique bleue et blanche et des gâteaux traditionnels au thé.

Nachdem die Hauptstadt 1868 nach Tokyo verlegt und 1945 der Adel abgeschafft wurde, verschwanden in Kyoto die meis-ten Adelswohnsitze. Yoshida Sanso, das ursprünglich für Prinz Higashi-Fushimi, dem Schwager des Showa-Kaisers Hirohito 1932 erbaut wurde, ist einer der wenigen, der noch erhalten ge-blieben ist. Das seit 1948 als ryokan (traditionelles Gästehaus) und Restaurant geführte Yoshida Sanso liegt nordöstlich von Kyoto in einem von alten Schreinen und Tempeln umgebenen Landstrich. Für seinen Bau verwendeten Zimmerleute edelstes Zypressenholz (hinoki) aus der Kiso-Region. Das ganz im Stil der 1930er-Jahre gehaltene Yoshida Sanso kann mit Art-Déco-Ele-menten im Vestibül und den oberen Räumen aufwarten. Die Be-sitzerin Kyoko Nakamura ist Kalligraphin, ihre Pinselmalereien zieren Schilder und Speisekarten. Während die Nakumaras den Originalcharakter des Adelswohnsitzes beibehalten, verwen-den sie ausgesuchte Accessoires wie Blumen, Kerzenständer, Tische, Tabletts und Geschirr, um ihm ein fürstliches Flair zu verleihen.

Le déplacement de la capitale à Tokyo en 1868, suivi par la destitution de l'aristocratie en 1945, sonna le glas des de-meures princières de Kyoto. Yoshida Sanso est l'une des rares restantes, construite en 1932 pour le prince Higashi-Fushimi, beau-frère de l'empereur Showa (Hirohito). Devenue ryokan (auberge traditionnelle) et restaurant en 1948, elle se trouve au nord-est de Kyoto dans un quartier entouré de vieux sanctuaires et de temples. Pour la construire, les charpentiers utilisèrent les plus beaux cèdres hinoki de la région de Kiso. Avec son vaste jardin, son haut portail et son allée incurvée, elle dégage une impression de grandeur et de délicatesse qui s'élève jusqu'aux détails des toits en cuivre. Reflétant le style des années trente, on y trouve des touches Art Déco telles que le lustre ou les vit-raux du vestibule et des chambres à l'étage. La propriétaire, Ky-oko Nakamura, est une calligraphe. Les Nakamura ont conservé l'aspect original de la demeure, choisissant soigneusement cha-que objet (fleurs, bougeoirs, tables, plateaux et vaisselle) pour créer une atmosphère de grâce princière.

LEFT ABOVE:
This purification basin is a study in water, stone, and bamboo.

LEFT BELOW:
Mother and daughter on the verandah.

RIGHT ABOVE:
Low-trimmed azalea bushes lead through the garden to the main hall, with delicately upward-turned roofs and windows hung with sudare (blinds) made of reeds.

RIGHT BELOW:
Purification water basin amidst bushes in the garden.

LINKS OBEN:
Dieses Reinigungsbecken wirkt wie ein Kunstwerk aus Wasser, Stein und Bambus.

LINKS UNTEN:
Mutter und Tochter auf der Veranda.

RECHTE SEITE OBEN:
Beschnittene Azaleen-büsche säumen den Weg zum Hauptgebäude, das über sanft nach oben geschwungene Dächer und Fenster mit Hänge-rollos (sudare) aus Binsen verfügt.

RECHTE SEITE UNTEN:
Ein Reinigungsbecken inmitten von Garten-sträuchern.

EN HAUT, À GAUCHE:
Ce bassin de purifica-tion est une composition d'eau, de pierre et de bambou.

EN BAS, À GAUCHE:
La mère et la fille sur la véranda.

PAGE DE DROITE, EN HAUT:
Dans le jardin, des buis-sons d'azalées taillés bas mènent au bâtiment principal, avec ses toits délicatement incurvés vers le ciel et ses fenêtres protégées de stores su-dare en roseaux.

PAGE DE DROITE, EN BAS:
Dans le jardin, un bassin de purification entre les buissons.

YOSHIDA SANSO / KYOTO

Chairs and table on the verandah, with sudare blinds allowing a view of the azalea garden. The balustrade is based on a variant of the Buddhist swastika pattern.

Veranda mit Tisch und Stühlen, von der aus man einen schönen Blick auf den Azaleengarten hat. Hängerollos (sudare) schützen vor der Sonne. Das Geländer weist eine Variation des buddhistischen Swastikamusters auf.

Des chaises et une table sur la véranda dominant le jardin d'azalées et protégée de stores sudare. La balustrade s'inspire d'une variante du svastika bouddhiste.

40

YOSHIDA SANSO / KYOTO

LEFT PAGE:
A gold lacquered soup bowl on a wooden tray, and Yoshida Sanso's house rice wine in a crystal glass bring a cool feeling to summer cuisine.

RIGHT PAGE:
Round table in second-floor room. Above is a stained-glass transom, with symbols representing the name of Prince Higashi-Fushimi, dating from the 1932 construction of the house.

LINKE SEITE:
Die goldlackierte Suppenschüssel auf dem hölzernen Tablett und das Kristallglas mit hauseigenem Reiswein von Yoshida Sanso verleihen der sommerlichen Cuisine etwas Erfrischendes.

RECHTE SEITE:
Ein runder Tisch im ersten Stock. Darüber ein Buntglasfenster mit dem Schriftzug Prinz Higashi-Fushimi. Es stammt noch von 1932, als das Haus errichtet wurde.

PAGE DE GAUCHE:
Le bol à soupe laqué or sur un plateau en bois et l'alcool de riz fait maison dans un verre en cristal apportent une note de fraîcheur dans la cuisine d'été.

42

PAGE DE DROITE:
Une table ronde dans la chambre à l'étage. L'imposte en vitrail avec le nom du prince Higashi-Fushimi date de 1932, quand la maison fut construite.

Dinner being served in the zashiki (main hall), with a tokonoma alcove to the left and a jodan (decorative corner) to the right, flanked by candle-sticks wrapped with rice paper.

Kyoto cuisine with seasonal motifs, in a wooden container in the shape of a treasure chest, beside some classic poetry written in calligraphy by the owner Kyoko Nakamura.

VORHERGEHENDE DOPPELSEITE:
Das Abendessen wird im Salon (zashiki) serviert, der links über eine Wandnische (tokonoma) und rechts über ein Zierbrett (jodan) verfügt. Gesäumt wird er von Kerzenständern mit Reispapierschirm.

Die saisonale Küche Kyotos, serviert in einem Holzbehälter, der an ein Schatzkästlein erinnert. Als Dreingabe ein kalligraphiertes klassisches Gedicht, handgeschrieben von der Eigentümerin Kyoko Nakamura.

46 DOUBLE PAGE PRÉCÉDENTE:
Le dîner est servi dans le zashiki (salon) avec une alcôve tokonoma à gauche et un jodan (coin décoratif) à droite, flanqué de torchères enveloppées dans du papier de riz.

La cuisine de Kyoto suit le rythme des saisons, ici présentée dans un coffret en bois et accompagnée d'un poème classique calligraphié par la propriétaire, Kyoko Nakamura.

YOSHIDA SANSO / KYOTO

PREVIOUS DOUBLE PAGE:
Room arranged for sleeping: bedding and iris screen beside glass doors, floor lamp, tray with water, and candle-stick with flaring rice-paper shade in front of tokonoma alcove.

LEFT PAGE:
Black lacquer desk with suzuri-bako (box for ink, brush, and inkstone), with bizen-ware jar and flower arrangement.

RIGHT PAGE:
Guest bedding, flanked by two-panel screen with iris painting. On the bed is a book with calligraphy by owner Kyoko Nakamura's father.

VORHERGEHENDE DOPPELSEITE:
Raum, der als Schlafzimmer hergerichtet wurde: Schlaflager und Stellschirm, eine Stehlampe sowie ein Kerzenständer mit Reispapierschirm vor einer Ziernische (tokonoma).

LINKE SEITE:
Schwarzer Lacktisch mit suzuri-bako (Schreibkasten mit Tusche, Pinseln und Tuschstein) sowie einem Bizen-Keramikkrug mit Blumenarrangement.

RECHTE SEITE:
Gästebett, flankiert von einem zweiteiligen Wandschirm mit Schwertlilienmotiv. Auf dem Bett liegt ein Buch mit Kalligraphien vom Vater der Eigentümerin Kyoko Nakamura.

DOUBLE PAGE PRÉCÉDENTE:
La chambre préparée pour la nuit : matelas et paravent orné d'iris masquant les portes en verre, bougeoir surmonté d'un abat-jour en papier de riz devant une alcôve tokonoma.

PAGE DE GAUCHE:
Bureau en laque noire avec un suzuri-bako (coffret contenant encre, brosse et pierre à encrer), ainsi qu'un vase en bizen et son arrangement floral.

PAGE DE DROITE:
Le lit d'amis, flanqué d'un paravent à deux feuilles orné d'iris. Sur le lit, un livre avec de calligraphies signée du père de Kyoko Nakamura, la propriétaire.

Tenmangu

ALEX KERR
KAMEOKA

Originally built as a nunnery in the early 1600's, the house was moved here to the grounds of a Shinto shrine in the mid-18th century. It's in typical Kyoto style: tiled roof, *tatami*-matted floors, sliding *fusuma* doors, and wooden drop ceilings. The old *doma*, or kitchen area, is still open to the rafters; in 1984 writer Alex Kerr remodeled this room as a calligraphy and writing studio. The rest of the house is basically in its original condition, decorated with Chinese and Japanese rugs and furniture, hanging scrolls and folding screens. The house was formerly the priest's home in the grounds of Yada-Tenmangu Shrine, in the town of Kameoka west of Kyoto. There are tens of thousands of Tenmangu shrines across Japan, all dedicated to the patron of calligraphy, literature, and scholarship. This house, where the writer has lived for thirty years, is ideally suited to a student of history and a lover of calligraphy.

Outer gate to the shrine precincts.

Äußeres Tor zum Schrein-gelände.

Portail s'ouvrant sur le sanctuaire.

Das im frühen 17. Jahrhundert ursprünglich für Nonnen errichtete Haus wurde Mitte des 18. Jahrhunderts auf das Gelände eines Shinto-Schreins versetzt. Es ist im typischen Kyoto-Stil gehalten, besitzt ein Ziegeldach, mit *tatami*-Matten ausgelegte Böden, Papierschiebetüren (*fusuma*) und niedrige Holzdecken. Das alte Erdgeschoss mit Küche, *doma* genannt, ist nach wie vor zum Dachstuhl hin offen. Im Jahr 1984 baute der Schriftsteller Alex Kerr diesen Raum um und machte ein Kalligraphie- und Schreibstudio daraus. Das restliche Haus wurde mehr oder weniger im Originalzustand belassen und ist mit chinesischen Teppichen und japanischen Möbeln, hängenden Schriftrollen und Stellschirmen eingerichtet. Das Haus war früher das Heim des Priesters der Yada-Tenmangu-Schreinanlage in der Stadt Kameoka, westlich von Kyoto. In ganz Japan gibt es zehntausende von Tenmangu-Schreinen, die alle dem Schutzpatron der Kalligraphie, Literatur und Gelehrsamkeit gewidmet sind. Für einen Liebhaber der Kalligraphie ist dieses Haus ideal geeignet.

Ce couvent du début du 17ᵉ siècle a été déplacé au milieu du 18ᵉ siècle sur le site d'un ancien temple shintoïste. Son style est typique de Kyoto : toit en tuiles, sols en *tatami*, *fusuma* (portes coulissantes) et plafonds en bois bordés de retombées. L'ancien *doma*, ou cuisine, est toujours ouvert jusqu'aux chevrons ; en 1984, l'écrivain Alex Kerr reconvertit cette pièce en sa salle de calligraphie et d'écriture. Le reste de la maison a plus ou moins conservé son état d'origine, décoré de tapis, de meubles chinois et japonais, de rouleaux et de paravents. Cette maison fut autrefois la résidence du prêtre du temple de Yada-Tenmangu, dans la ville de Kameoka à l'ouest de Kyoto. Il existe des dizaines de milliers de temples Tenmangu éparpillés dans tout le Japon, tous consacrés au maître de la calligraphie, de la littérature et de l'érudition. Pour Alex Kerr, féru d'histoire et grand amateur de calligraphie, cette demeure qu'il habite depuis trente ans, lui semblait toute destinée.

LEFT:
Edo period (1603-1868) stone lantern by the walkway to the shrine.

RIGHT ABOVE:
Pebble-filled tsukubai (purification basin).

RIGHT BELOW:
Autumnal maples among the ancient roots and stones of the Tenmangu garden.

LINKE SEITE:
Steinlaterne aus der Edo-Zeit (1603–1868) am Weg-rand zum Schrein.

RECHTS OBEN:
Kiesgefülltes Reinigungs-becken (tsukubai).

RECHTS UNTEN:
Herbstlich verfärbtes Ahornlaub zwischen alten Baumwurzeln und Steinen im Tenmangu-Garten.

PAGE DE GAUCHE:
Lanterne en pierre de la période Edo (1603-1868) au bord de l'allée menant au sanctuaire.

EN HAUT, À DROITE:
Tsukubai (basin de purifi-cation) rempli de galets.

EN BAS, À DROITE:
Érables automnaux parmi les racines et les pierres anciennes du jardin de Tenmangu.

55

TENMANGU / KAMEOKA

In the main room, an
incense burner and spirit
stone on a Qing Chinese
table; andon floor lamps,
one papered with bunraku
puppet theatre script, sit
on nabeshima rugs.

*Im Salon ein chinesischer
Tisch aus der Qing-Dynas-
tie mit einem Räucherge-
fäß und einem spirituellen
Stein. Daneben Stehlam-
pen (andon), von denen
eine mit einem bunra-
ku-Puppentheaterskript
bezogen wurde.*

*Dans la pièce principa-
le, encadrant un brûleur
d'encens et une pierre
« esprit » sur une table
chinoise Qing, des lam-
padaires andon, dont un
portant des écritures de
théâtre de marionnettes
bunraku.*

4 x 4 House

BY TADAO ANDO FOR YOSHINORI NAKATA
AKASHI, HYOGO

Tadao Ando has gained international renown as the architect of abstract spaces formed from bare concrete slabs. Nowhere is his concept so simple as in the 4 x 4 House, a small
tower at the edge of the Inland Sea. Each floor measures
4 x 4 meters, hence the name. Built in 2003 for architect and
property developer Yoshinori Nakata, the house consists of four
stories and a basement, each with only one room dedicated to
a single function: entry hall, bedroom, study, and living/dining-
room. In Ando's Church of the Light outside Osaka, he pierced
a bare wall with a tall cross – thus turning a concrete slab into
a choir screen through which shines the light of the divine. In
the 4 x 4 House, Ando again surprises us. Spartan though the
layout appears to be, the house rises to an offset upper cube, at
which point it achieves epiphany. Here, a double-story expanse
of plate glass covering the seaside face of the cube reveals a
breathtaking view of the Inland Sea and nearby Akashi Bridge.

Wooden model of the 4 x 4 House.

Holzmodell des 4 x 4 House.

Maquette en bois de la maison 4 x 4.

Tadao Ando genießt als Architekt abstrakter Gebäude aus Beton internationale Anerkennung. Nirgendwo ist sein Konzept so schlicht wie beim 4 x 4 House, einem kleinen Turm am Rande der Inlandsee. Jedes Stockwerk misst 4 x 4 Meter, daher der Name. Das 2003 für den Architekten und Bauunternehmer Yoshinori Nakata errichtete Haus hat vier Stockwerke und ein Souterrain, die jeweils aus einem einzigen Raum bestehen, der ausschließlich eine Funktion erfüllt: Flur, Schlafzimmer, Arbeitszimmer und Wohn-/Esszimmer. In Andos „Church of Light" außerhalb von Osaka durchbrach er eine nackte Betonwand mit einem großen Kreuz. Auf diese Weise verwandelte er eine Betonplatte in eine Chorschranke, durch die das Licht des Göttlichen scheint. Auch beim 4 x 4 House wartet Ando mit einer Überraschung auf: Obwohl der Entwurf spartanisch wirkt, endet das Haus oben in einen versetzten Würfel – die reinste Offenbarung. Hier bietet eine Scheibe aus Bauglas, das zwei zur See gewandte Stockwerke bedeckt, eine atemberaubende Aussicht auf die Inlandsee und die nahe gelegene Akashi-Brücke.

Tadao Ando s'est forgé une réputation internationale d'architecte des espaces abstraits créés avec des dalles de béton brut. La maison 4 x 4, une petite tour au bord de la mer Intérieure, illustre à merveille ce concept. Chaque étage mesure 4 mètres sur 4, d'où son nom. Construite en 2003 pour l'architecte et promoteur immobilier Yoshinori Nakata, elle possède quatre étages et un sous-sol, chacun servant une fonction unique : vestibule, chambre, bureau, séjour/salle à manger. Dans l'Eglise de la lumière qu'il a bâtie près d'Osaka, Ando a percé un mur nu d'une haute croix, transformant ainsi une paroi de béton en fond de chœur par où filtre la lumière divine. Dans la maison 4 x 4, il nous surprend encore. Bien que le plan paraisse spartiate, la structure est couronnée d'un cube légèrement décentré ; là vous attend la révélation. Avec sa double hauteur sous plafond, la pièce est bordée d'un mur vitré qui offre une vue à couper le souffle sur la mer Intérieure et le pont Akashi voisin.

LEFT:
The upper cube of the concrete tower is offset one meter to the east; steps descend to a concrete stage that disappears under seawater at high tide.

RIGHT ABOVE:
Window on the third level looking out to the Inland Sea and the Akashi Bridge.

RIGHT BELOW:
The ladder from the fourth floor, looking down from the loft.

LINKE SEITE:
Der obere Würfel des Betonturms ist um einen Meter nach Osten verschoben. Stufen führen zu einer Betonplattform hinunter, die bei Flut unter dem Meerwasser verschwindet.

RECHTS OBEN:
Die Fenster im zweiten Stock gehen auf die Inlandsee und die Akashi-Brücke hinaus.

RECHTS UNTEN:
Die Leiter zum dritten Stock, vom Loft aus gesehen.

PAGE DE GAUCHE:
Le cube supérieur de la tour en béton est décalé d'un mètre vers l'Est. Les marches descendent vers une terrasse en béton à moitié submergée à marée haute.

EN HAUT, À DROITE:
Les fenêtres du troisième étage donnent sur la mer Intérieure et le pont Akashi.

EN BAS, À DROITE:
Au quatrième étage, l'échelle qui mène au grenier.

A window in Tadao Ando's trademark unfinished reinforced concrete wall, with a wide sheet of glass affording a panorama of the Inland Sea from the kitchen and dining room.

Ein Fenster, eingelassen in der für Tadao Ando typischen, unbehandelten Stahlbetonwand sowie ein riesiges Panoramafenster sorgen in Küche und Esszimmer für einen unverstellten Blick auf die Inlandsee.

Dans la cuisine/salle à manger, la baie vitrée et la fenêtre percée dans le mur en béton brut, typique du style de Tadao Ando, offrent une vue panoramique sur la mer Intérieure.

62

64

LEFT ABOVE:
The kitchen, seen from above, with a landward view from the window.

LEFT BELOW:
Ando designed most of the cabinetwork and furniture.

RIGHT ABOVE:
Table, chairs, wooden floor, sand, and sea.

RIGHT BELOW:
Kitchen cabinets designed by Ando.

LINKS OBEN:
Die Küche von oben, mit Ausblick ins Landesinnere.

LINKS UNTEN:
Ando entwarf auch ein Großteil der Schränke und Möbel.

RECHTE SEITE OBEN:
Tisch, Stühle, Holzboden, der Strand und das Meer.

RECHTE SEITE UNTEN:
Küchenschränke im Ando-Design.

EN HAUT, À GAUCHE:
La cuisine vue du haut, avec une fenêtre donnant sur la ville.

EN BAS, À GAUCHE:
Ando a dessiné la plupart des meubles.

PAGE DE DROITE, EN HAUT:
Une table, des chaises, un parquet, du sable et la mer.

PAGE DE DROITE, EN BAS:
Les placards de la cuisine dessinés par Ando.

4 X 4 HOUSE / AKASHI – HYOGO

Go'o Shrine

BY HIROSHI SUGIMOTO
NAOSHIMA ISLAND, KAGAWA

The small island of Naoshima in the Inland Sea is a living museum. Billionaire Soichiro Fukutake built Benesse House, a resort hotel surrounding an art museum, and then proceeded to embellish the island with another gallery, and artworks by contemporary artists placed strategically along roads and beaches. As part of this process, the Art House Project, founded in 1998, invites world artists to build installations on the sites of old buildings. Go'o Shrine, designed by photographer Hiroshi Sugimoto, re-interprets the traditional Shinto shrine in new form. The white gravel enclosure and the simple lines of the pillars and straight roofs conjure the pure mystery of Ise Shrine, Japan's holiest, which Sugimoto studied and photographed. The glass steps, which appear modern, reflect back in time and space to the world of ancient burial mounds. Flowing far underground, the steps bring light from the shrine into the depths of the earth, linking the space of light and life above with ancestral spirits of the land.

The original stone steps, covered with high-quality optical glass, chosen for its flawlessness and transparency, descend to the foot of the granite pediment.

Die Originalsteinstufen, die mit hochwertigem optischem Glas bedeckt sind, das wegen seiner Makellosigkeit und Transparenz ausgewählt wurde, führen den Granitsockel hinab.

Les marches en pierre d'origine, recouvertes d'un verre optique de grande qualité choisi pour sa perfection et sa transparence, descendent jusqu'au pied du porche en granit.

Die kleine Insel Naoshima in der Inlandsee ist ein lebendiges Museum. Der Milliardär Soichiro Fukutake ließ erst das Benesse House errichten, eine Hotelanlage mit Kunstmuseum, und schenkte der Insel anschließend noch eine weitere Galerie sowie diverse Werke zeitgenössischer Künstler, die an Straßen und Stränden strategisch platziert wurden. Teil dieses Konzepts ist das 1998 gegründete Art House Project, das Künstler aus aller Welt einlädt, Installationen auf dem Gelände alter Gebäude zu errichten. Der Go'o Shrine, der von dem Fotografen Hiroshi Sugimoto entworfen wurde, ist eine moderne Interpretation des traditionellen Shinto-Schreins. Die Einfriedung mit weißem Kies, die nüchternen Säulen und das geradlinige Dach beschwören das Geheimnis des Schreins von Ise, der wichtigsten Kultstätte Japans, die Sugimoto ausgiebig studiert und fotografiert hat. Die Glasstufen, die nur auf den ersten Blick modern wirken, führen in die Vergangenheit und bringen das Licht des Schreins in die Tiefen der Erde. So verbinden sie das darüber liegende Reich des Lichts mit den uralten Geistern des Landes.

La petite île de Naoshima dans la mer Intérieure est un musée vivant. Le richissime Soichiro Fukutake y a construit Benesse, un complexe hôtelier entourant un musée d'art, avant d'embellir l'île d'une autre galerie et d'œuvres d'artistes contemporains placées stratégiquement le long des routes et des plages. L' Art House Project, fondé en 1998, invite des artistes internationaux à construire des installations sur les sites de bâtiments anciens. Parmi elles, le temple Go'o, conçu par le photographe Hiroshi Sugimoto, réinterprète le sanctuaire shinto. La cour fermée en gravier blanc et les lignes simples des colonnes et des toits plats évoquent le mystère du temple Ise, le plus sacré du Japon, que Sugimoto a étudié et photographié. Les marches en verre, faussement modernes, renvoient au monde des anciens tumulus funéraires. Elles apportent la lumière du temple dans les profondeurs de la terre, reliant la vie et l'air de la surface aux esprits ancestraux souterrains.

LEFT ABOVE:
Stone steps, overlaid with glass, lead from the haiden (worship hall) to the honden (main sanctuary).

LEFT BELOW:
The glass steps continue into the underground Stone Chamber, a crypt-like structure below the worship hall, where light enters to create a virtual stairway to heaven.

RIGHT:
The haiden, or worship hall, frames the steps originally of stone and now covered with glass. A field of white pebbles, marking the sacred enclosure, surrounds the shrine.

LINKS OBEN:
Mit Glas bedeckte Steinstufen führen von der Haupthalle des Schreins (haiden) zum Hauptheiligtum (honden).

LINKS UNTEN:
Die Glasstufen setzen sich bis in die unterirdische Steinkammer fort, ein Krypta-ähnlicher Raum unter der Haupthalle, in den Licht fällt und eine Art virtuelle Treppe zum Himmel bildet.

RECHTE SEITE:
Der haiden, die Haupthalle, beschirmt die Stufen, die ursprünglich aus Stein waren und nun mit Glas beschichtet sind. Ein Bett aus weißem Kies umgibt den heiligen Schrein.

EN HAUT, À GAUCHE:
Des marches en pierre recouvertes de verre mènent du haiden (salle de culte) au honden (sanctuaire principal).

EN BAS, À GAUCHE:
Les marches en verre descendent jusque dans la crypte sous la salle du culte, où la lumière crée un escalier virtuel vers le ciel.

PAGE DE DROITE:
On accède au haiden, salle du culte, par d'anciennes marches en pierre à présent recouvertes de verre. Un champ de galets blancs délimite l'aire sacrée du sanctuaire.

GO'O SHRINE / NAOSHIMA ISLAND - KAGAWA

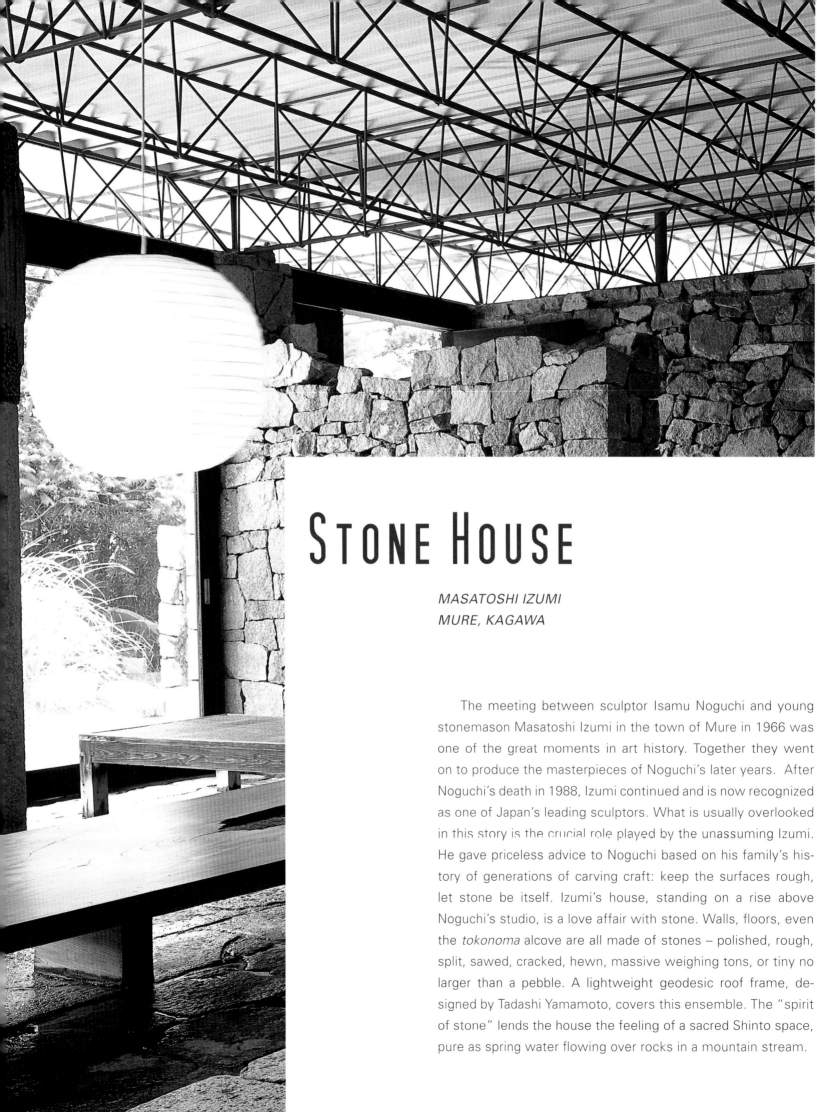

STONE HOUSE

MASATOSHI IZUMI
MURE, KAGAWA

The meeting between sculptor Isamu Noguchi and young stonemason Masatoshi Izumi in the town of Mure in 1966 was one of the great moments in art history. Together they went on to produce the masterpieces of Noguchi's later years. After Noguchi's death in 1988, Izumi continued and is now recognized as one of Japan's leading sculptors. What is usually overlooked in this story is the crucial role played by the unassuming Izumi. He gave priceless advice to Noguchi based on his family's history of generations of carving craft: keep the surfaces rough, let stone be itself. Izumi's house, standing on a rise above Noguchi's studio, is a love affair with stone. Walls, floors, even the *tokonoma* alcove are all made of stones – polished, rough, split, sawed, cracked, hewn, massive weighing tons, or tiny no larger than a pebble. A lightweight geodesic roof frame, designed by Tadashi Yamamoto, covers this ensemble. The "spirit of stone" lends the house the feeling of a sacred Shinto space, pure as spring water flowing over rocks in a mountain stream.

Walls and floors are made from aji-ishi, a fine granite from nearby quarries. Isamu Noguchi designed the paper lanterns, known as akari, and advised on the lightweight steel-trussed ceiling.

Wände und Böden sind aus aji-ishi, einem feinen Granit aus den nahe gelegenen Steinbrüchen. Isamu Noguchi entwarf die Papierlaternen namens akari und beriet bei der Stahlgitterdecke in Leichtbauweise.

Les murs et les sols sont en aji-ishi, un beau granit extrait des carrières voisines. Les lanternes en papier sont d'Isamu Noguchi, qui a également été consulté pour la structure légère en acier du plafond.

Die Begegnung des Bildhauers Isamu Noguchi mit dem jungen Steinmetz Masatoshi Izumi 1966 in der Stadt Mure markiert einen bedeutenden Moment in der Kunstgeschichte. Gemeinsam schufen Sie das Spätwerk von Noguchi. Nachdem Noguchi 1988 starb, setzte Izumi seine Arbeit fort und zählt heute zu den größten Bildhauern Japans. Dabei wird die Leistung des bescheidenen Izumi nur allzu oft übersehen. Er stammt aus einer Familie, die sich bereits seit Generationen der Steinbearbeitung verschrieben hat, und machte Noguchi ein unbezahlbares Geschenk für dessen Skulpturen: Er beließ die Oberflächen rau, um auf diese Weise den Charakter des Steins zu bewahren. Izumis Haus, das an einem Hang über Noguchis Atelier liegt, ist eine Liebeserklärung an den Stein. Wände, Böden, ja sogar die tokonoma (Alkoven), sie alle bestehen aus Stein – sei er nun poliert, rau, rissig, gesägt, behauen, tonnenschwer oder gerade einmal kieselsteingroß. Die „Seele des Steins" verleiht dem Haus die Atmosphäre eines heiligen Shinto-Schreins, so rein wie Quellwasser, das über Felsen strömt.

La rencontre du sculpteur Isamu Noguchi et du jeune tailleur de pierre Masatoshi Izumi à Mure en 1966 marqua un tournant dans l'histoire de l'art. Ensemble, ils créèrent les chefs-d'œuvre des dernières années de Noguchi. Après la mort du maître en 1988, le discret Izumi poursuivit sa carrière pour devenir aujourd'hui l'un des plus grands sculpteurs du Japon. On oublie trop souvent son rôle crucial. Il a apporté à Noguchi le précieux don de la taille, cultivé par sa famille pendant des générations : celui de respecter les surfaces brutes et de laisser la pierre parler d'elle-même. Sa maison, perchée sur une colline au-dessus de l'atelier de Noguchi, est un chant d'amour à la gloire de la pierre. Les murs, les sols et même le tokonoma (alcôve) sont en pierre : polie, brute, fendue, sciée, craquelée, taillée, massive et lourde ou pas plus grosse qu'un galet. La structure est couverte d'un toit géodésique dessiné par Tadashi Yamamoto. « L'esprit de la pierre » confère à la maison l'atmosphère d'un temple shinto, aussi pure que l'eau de source qui s'écoule sur les cailloux dans un ruisseau de montagne.

72

LEFT ABOVE:
The triangular roof over
a stone rectangle make
an Isamu Noguchi-style
geometrical arrangement.
Light pours out from the
glass-lined steel-trussed
gap between wall and
ceiling.

LEFT BELOW:
Izumi never wastes a
single piece of stone.
Unused fragments from
his atelier stand piled up
in the front garden, with
grasses growing freely,
nature reclaiming man's
work.

RIGHT ABOVE:
Mossy old stones from
ancient lanterns and
shrine carvings sit with
newer fragments in the
back garden.

RIGHT BELOW:
Fourth-generation Masa-
toshi Izumi splits stones
to reveal their inner souls.
Polished internal surfaces
contrast with the skin of
rough-textured boulders.

LINKE SEITE OBEN:
Das dreieckige Sattel-
dach über dem Stein-
rechteck bildet ein für
Isamu Noguchi typisches
geometrisches Arrange-
ment. Licht dringt aus
dem glaseingefassten,
metallgittergestützten
Raum zwischen Wänden
und Decke.

LINKE SEITE UNTEN:
Izumi hat kein einziges
Stück Stein verschwen-
det. Unbenutzte Frag-
mente aus seinem Atelier
türmen sich im Vorgarten,
wo das Gras wild wach-
sen darf und das von Men-
schenhand geschaffene
Werk zurückerobert.

RECHTS OBEN:
Im Garten hinter dem
Haus liegen bemooste alte
Steine, die von antiken La-
ternen und Schreinreliefs
stammen, neben neueren
Fragmenten.

RECHTS UNTEN:
Masatoshi Izumi, Stein-
metz in der vierten Ge-
neration, spaltete Steine,
um ihr Innenleben zu
offenbaren. Polierte Innen-
flächen kontrastieren mit
dem rauen Äußeren der
Felsbrocken.

PAGE DE GAUCHE, EN HAUT:
Le toit triangulaire posé
sur un rectangle de pierre
forme un arrangement
géométrique propre au
style d'Isamu Noguchi. La
lumière filtre par l'espace
vitré entre les murs et le
plafond.

PAGE DE GAUCHE, EN BAS:
Avec Izumi, rien ne se
perd. Des fragments de
pierre inutilisés provenant
de son atelier sont empi-
lés dans le jardin devant la
maison et envahis par les
herbes, la nature repre-
nant ses droits.

EN HAUT, À DROITE:
Derrière la maison, de
vieilles pierres envahies
par la mousse, provenant
d'anciennes lanternes et
de sanctuaires, côtoient
des fragments plus ré-
cents.

EN BAS, À DROITE:
Depuis quatre généra-
tions, la famille d'Izumi
fend la pierre pour révéler
son âme. Les surfaces
internes polies contrastent
avec la texture rugueuse
des rochers.

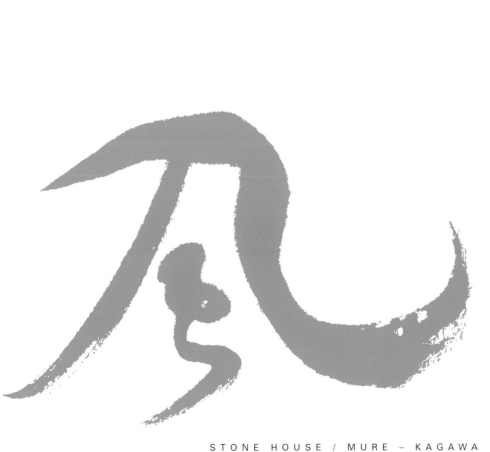

STONE HOUSE / MURE – KAGAWA

LEFT PAGE:
Corner of the reception room. Grasses grow from interstices in the wall where larger blocks are fitted together with smaller pieces. A pot holds wildflowers from the garden.

RIGHT PAGE:
Stone, bamboo, paper, and tatami frame the view from the front garden to the back garden, through the tokonoma alcove room.

FOLLOWING DOUBLE PAGE:
A table made from a huge log is the centerpiece of the reception room. Massive boulders rise as walls, and granite slabs, sprinkled with water to receive guests, form the floor.

LINKE SEITE:
Ein Ausschnitt aus dem Empfangsraum. Dort, wo größere Blöcke auf kleinere Steine treffen, sprießen Gräser aus Mauerritzen. Eine Vase enthält Wildblumen aus dem Garten.

RECHTE SEITE:
Stein, Bambus, Papier und Binsenmatten (tatami) bilden einen schönen Rahmen für den Blick in den rückwärtigen Garten. Davor sieht man den Raum mit der traditionellen Wandnische (tokonoma).

FOLGENDE DOPPELSEITE:
Ein Tisch aus einem riesigen Baumstamm ist der Blickfang des Empfangsraums. Gewaltige Felsbrocken bilden die Wände, während der Boden aus Granitblöcken besteht, die für den Besuch mit Wasser besprenkelt wurden.

PAGE DE GAUCHE:
Un coin de la réception. L'herbe pousse dans les interstices entre les pierres de différentes tailles. Dans un pot, des fleurs sauvages du jardin.

PAGE DE DROITE:
Dans l'alcôve tokonoma, une composition de pierre, bambou, papier et tatami encadre la vue sur le jardin.

DOUBLE PAGE SUIVANTE:
Une table taillée dans un énorme tronc au centre de la réception. Les murs sont montés avec des rochers massifs tandis que le sol est en dalles de granit, ici aspergées d'eau pour accueillir les invités.

74

STONE HOUSE / MURE – KAGAWA

Chiiori

ALEX KERR AND MASON FLORENCE
IYA, TOKUSHIMA

Chiiori is a thatched farmhouse in Iya Valley, on the island of Shikoku. Iya, with Japan's deepest mountain gorges, was a place of refuge where defeated warriors fled at the end of the 12th century. Even now it is a remote place, with thatched houses perched high over chasms from which boil up clouds and mist. Writer Alex Kerr bought the house in 1973, naming it Chiiori, which means "Cottage of the Flute." In 1997, Mason Florence became part-owner. The house is not a large structure, but the lack of walls or ceilings means that the interior makes up one vast cathedral-like space. Built in the early 18th century, Chiiori has a roof thatched with *kaya* (long-leaved miscanthus reeds), and three floor hearths *(irori)*, around which the inhabitants sit for cooking and for warmth in the winter. After hundreds of years of smoke rising from the *irori* hearths, the interior of the house has darkened, so that the beams, pillars, even the floors have turned a shiny black, called in old Japanese "black glistening."

Under the verandah is stored a winter supply of logs for the irori (hearths), floor and roof tiles come from an old Kyoto kura storehouse.

Unter der Veranda werden der Wintervorrat Brennholz für die in den Boden eingelassenen Feuerstellen (irori) sowie Dachziegel eines alten Kyotoer Lagerhauses (kura) aufbewahrt.

Sous la véranda, la réserve de bois pour l'hiver destinée aux foyers irori dans le sol, aménagés et des tuiles provenant d'un vieil entrepôt kura de Kyoto.

Chiiori ist ein strohgedecktes Bauernhaus im Iya-Tal auf der Insel Shikoku. Das Tal mit Japans tiefsten Bergschluchten war gegen Ende des 12. Jahrhunderts ein Zufluchtsort für besiegte Krieger. Noch heute ist es sehr abgelegen mit seinen strohgedeckten Häusern, die hoch über den Schluchten hängen, von denen Wolken und Nebel aufsteigen. Der Schriftsteller Alex Kerr kaufte das Haus 1973 und nannte es Chiiori, was „Haus der Flöte" bedeutet. Im Jahr 1997 wurde Mason Florence zum Miteigentümer. Das Haus ist nicht besonders groß, aber da es keine Zwischenwände und Zwischendecken hat, wirkt sein Inneres wie eine riesige Kathedrale. Das im frühen 18. Jahrhundert errichtete Chiiori hat ein Dach, das mit *kaya* (Schilfgras) gedeckt ist, sowie drei im Boden eingelassene Feuerstellen *(irori)*. Um die versammeln sich die Bewohner zum Kochen oder um sich im Winter aufzuwärmen. Nachdem jahrhundertelang Rauch von den *irori* aufstieg, ist das Hausinnere geschwärzt, sodass Balken, Pfeiler, ja sogar die Böden schwarz geworden sind.

Chiiori est une ferme au toit en chaume dans la vallée d'Iya, sur l'île de Shikoku. Iya, qui abrite les gorges les plus profondes du Japon, servit de refuge aux guerriers vaincus à la fin du 12e siècle. Aujourd'hui encore, c'est un lieu isolé avec des cabanes couvertes de chaume perchées au bord de précipices d'où s'élèvent des nuages et de la brume. Alex Kerr acheta cette maison en 1973, la baptisant Chiiori, la « maisonnette de la flûte ». En 1997, Mason Florence en devint copropriétaire. La structure est petite mais, du fait de l'absence de murs et de plafonds, on se croirait à l'intérieur d'une vaste cathédrale. Construite au début du 18e siècle, Chiiori a un toit en *kaya* (roseau de Chine) et trois *irori* (foyers creusés dans le sol) autour desquels on s'assoit pour cuisiner ou se réchauffer l'hiver. Après des siècles d'usage, la fumée des *irori* a noirci les poutres, les colonnes et même les sols, leur donnant ce que les Japonais appelle «un lustre noir».

82

PREVIOUS DOUBLE PAGE:
The interior of the house is one large open space, lit by andon lamps reflected on smooth blackened floorboards. Mushiro straw mats surround the sunken hearths.

LEFT:
A black tile-ware container, used for storing coals from the hearth, on a lacquered table. The banner in the background features a triple oakleaf samurai crest.

RIGHT:
The flaming irori hearths are the center of life in the house. Smoke rising from the irori has blackened the floors, pillars, and rafters over hundreds of years.

VORIGE DOPPELSEITE:
Das Innere des Hauses ist ein großer, offener Raum. Stehlampen (andon) spenden Licht, das sich in den polierten, geschwärzten Holzdielen spiegelt. Strohmatten (mushiro) umgeben die Feuerstellen.

LINKE SEITE:
Ein schwarz glasiertes Tongefäß zur Aufbewahrung von Kohle auf einem Lacktisch. Den Wandbehang im Hintergrund schmückt ein Samurai-Wappen.

RECHTE SEITE:
Die in den Boden eingelassenen, lodernden Feuerstellen (irori) bilden den Lebensmittelpunkt des Hauses. Der davon aufsteigende Rauch hat die Böden, Balken und Dachsparren über Jahrhunderte geschwärzt.

DOUBLE PAGE PRÉCÉDENTE:
L'intérieur est un grand espace ouvert éclairé par des andon qui se reflètent dans le parquet lisse et noirci. Des paillasses mushiro entourent les foyers creusés dans le sol.

PAGE DE GAUCHE:
Un récipient noir en ardoise servant à recueillir des braises, posé sur une table laquée. La bannière représente des armoiries samouraï.

PAGE DE DROITE:
Les foyers irori constituent le cœur de la maison. Au fil des siècles, leur fumée a noirci les sols, les colonnes et les poutres.

86

HOUSE OF LIGHT

BY JAMES TURRELL AND DAIGO ISHII
TOKAMACHI, NIIGATA

Artist James Turrell is known worldwide as "the artist of light." His artworks take time to experience, time to take in the passage of time and changing shades of light. So in 2000, as part of the First Echigo-Tsumari Triennial art event in Niigata Prefecture near the Japan Sea coast, Turrell designed an inn where one can spend a day and a night enveloped in his world of light and shadow. Architect Daigo Ishii designed the building in Japanese style with *tatami*-matted rooms, wooden-floored corridors, verandahs, and *yukimi-shoji*, paper doors with cut-out windows for viewing the deep snow for which the Niigata region is known. Into these traditional surroundings, Turrell brought soft overhead lighting in various hues. The "Outside-In" room features an aperture that slides open to the sky, surrounded by a computer-coordinated ceiling that changes color as sunset progresses. At night, the house comes into its own, as stairways, doorframes, and even the edges of the bath glow with surreal light.

Stairway leading to the second floor bathed in light from the skyspace above.

Die Treppe in den ersten Stock wird durch den darüber gelegenen „Skyspace" in Licht getaucht.

Une lucarne dans le plafond illumine l'escalier.

Der Künstler James Turrell ist weltweit als Lichtkünstler berühmt. Um seine Kunstwerke zu begreifen, muss man sich Zeit nehmen – Zeit, um das Verstreichen der Zeit und das sich verändernde Licht zu begreifen. Als er 2000 von der Niigata-Präfektur an die Küste des Japanischen Meers eingeladen wurde, entwarf Turrell ein Gästehaus, wo man einen Tag und eine Nacht in seiner Welt aus Licht und Schatten verbringen kann. Der Architekt Daigo Ishii entwarf das Gebäude im japanischen Stil: Räume, die mit *tatami*-Matten ausgelegt sind, Flure aus Holzdielen, Veranden und *yukimi-shoji*, Papiertüren mit ausgesparten Fenstern, durch die man die tief verschneite Landschaft betrachten kann, für die die Niigata-Präfektur so berühmt ist. In diese traditionelle Umgebung integrierte Turrell eine sanfte Deckenbeleuchtung in verschiedenen Farbschattierungen. Der „Outside-In-Room" verfügt über eine zur Seite gleitende Fensterblende, die den Blick auf den Himmel freigibt, umgeben von einer computergesteuerten Decke, die ihre Farbe während des Sonnenuntergangs verändert.

James Turrell est connu dans le monde entier comme «l'artiste de la lumière». Il faut du temps pour apprécier ses œuvres, celui de suivre le passage du temps et les nuances changeantes de la lumière. C'est pourquoi, invité en 2000 par la préfecture de Niigata, il a conçu une auberge près de la mer du Japon où l'on peut s'immerger une journée et une nuit dans son monde d'ombres et de lumière. L'architecte Daigo Ishii a construit le bâtiment dans le style japonais avec des pièces tapissées de *tatamis*, des couloirs en parquet, des vérandas, des *yukimi-shoji*, des portes en papier percées de fenêtres donnant sur l'épais tapis de neige qui fait la réputation de la région. Dans cet environnement traditionnel, Turrell a créé un éclairage par le haut tout en nuances changeantes. Le plafond de la pièce « Dehors-dedans », qu'un ordinateur fait changer de couleur à mesure que le soleil se couche, possède une trappe coulissante qui s'ouvre sur le ciel. La nuit, l'escalier, les cadres de portes et même le bord de la baignoire luisent d'une lumière surnaturelle, révélant la maison dans toute sa splendeur.

Constructed in traditional sukiya style, with a pillared verandah and gently slanting gabled and hipped roofs, the House of Light glows against the darkening sky.

Das im traditionellen sukiya-Stil gehaltene House of Light mit seiner auf Säulen ruhenden Veranda und den leicht schrägen Walmdächern leuchtet in der Dämmerung.

Construite dans le style sukiya traditionnel avec une véranda bordée de colonnes et des toits à pignons peu pentus, la maison luit à la tombée du soir.

90

LEFT:
A skyspace illuminating the entry to the bath, and a blue light around the perimeter, are mirrored in still water.

RIGHT:
Light from the colonnaded interior cascades down the grand exterior staircase.

LINKE SEITE:
Das den Eingang zum Bad beleuchtende Oberlicht sowie das blaue Licht der Beckeneinfassung spiegeln sich im Wasser.

RECHTE SEITE:
Licht aus den auf Säulen ruhenden Innenräumen fließt die große Außentreppe hinab.

PAGE DE GAUCHE:
L'ouverture dans le toit et la lumière bleue qui borde le bain se reflètent dans l'eau.

PAGE DE DROITE:
La lumière de l'espace intérieur dévale le grand escalier extérieur.

92

96

PREVIOUS DOUBLE PAGE LEFT:
Yellow light from the ceiling and light from outside shining through the shoji doors reflect on the wooden floors of the entryway.

PREVIOUS DOUBLE PAGE RIGHT:
Golden-lit doors of the first-floor corridor look out onto gravel, stepping stones, and the trees beyond.

LEFT ABOVE:
Wooden stool and bucket beside the bath in daylight.

LEFT BELOW
Black gravel, large white and small black pebbles, and a straight border delineate the perimeter.

RIGHT ABOVE:
Key to James Turrell's image of the house is the concept "Outside In." Here, the bath inside basks in morning light from the outside.

RIGHT BELOW:
The ocher-painted surface of the ground floor walls glows red under evening light.

VORIGE DOPPELSEITE LINKS:
Die gelbe Deckenbeleuchtung sowie das Tageslicht, das durch die papierbespannten Türen (shoji) fällt, spiegelt sich in den Holzdielen des Eingangsbereichs.

VORIGE DOPPELSEITE RECHTS:
Die golden angestrahlten Türen im Flur des Erdgeschosses gehen auf Kies, einen Natursteinweg und Bäume hinaus.

LINKS OBEN:
Schemel und Eimer aus Holz neben dem Wasserbecken bei Tageslicht.

LINKS UNTEN:
Schwarzer Kies, große weiße und kleine schwarze Kiesel sowie eine geradlinige Einfassung säumen das Grundstück.

RECHTE SEITE OBEN:
Ein wesentlicher Bestandteil von James Turrells Idee für das Haus ist sein „Outside In"-Konzept. Auf diesem Foto wird das Bad im Gebäudeinnern durch die von draußen hereinscheinende Morgensonne erhellt.

RECHTE SEITE UNTEN:
Die ockerfarben gestrichenen Wände im Erdgeschoss leuchten rot im Abendlicht.

DOUBLE PAGE PRÉCÉDENTE, A GAUCHE:
L'éclairage jaune du plafond et la lumière extérieure filtrée par les portes shoji se reflètent dans le parquet de l'entrée.

DOUBLE PAGE PRÉCÉDENTE, A DROITE:
Les portes du couloir, illuminées d'or, s'ouvrent sur le gravier, les pierres de gué et les arbres.

EN HAUT, À GAUCHE:
Un tabouret et un seau en bois au bord du bain.

EN BAS, À GAUCHE:
Du gravillon noir, des galets blancs et des cailloux noirs dessinent des lignes droites qui délimitent la cour.

PAGE DE DROITE, EN HAUT:
Le concept de James Turrell consiste à faire entrer l'extérieur à l'intérieur de la maison. Ici, le bain intérieur est inondé de lumière matinale.

PAGE DE DROITE, EN BAS:
Les murs ocre du rez-de-chaussée se teignent de rouge dans la lumière du soir.

HOUSE OF LIGHT / TOKAMACHI – NIIGATA

Guest bedding in what appears to be a traditional Japanese room, but is actually under a retractable skyspace that opens slowly for observing the sky at night.

Ein Gästeschlaflager in einem vermeintlich traditionellen japanischen Zimmer. Doch es befindet sich genau unter einem Oberlicht, das sich nachts langsam öffnet, um den Blick auf den Sternenhimmel freizugeben.

Dans la chambre d'amis au décor faussement traditionnel, le plafond s'ouvre lentement sur une vue du ciel nocturne.

ONE GRAIN OF
COOKED RICE
ONE SPOONFUL
OF TEARS
GRIND UNTIL
PASTE.
WITH THE PASTE
FILL THE SPACE
UNDER THE NAIL
OF THE SMALL
FINGER OF
THE RIGHT
HAND

MIX
FRESH MILK
FROM
THE BREAST
WITH

WASH YOUR
BEDSHEETS

DREAM HOUSE

BY MARINA ABRAMOVICH
TOKAMACHI, NIIGATA

Belgrade-born performance artist Marina Abramovich is no-
torious for pushing the limits – to the point of putting herself in
mortal peril in the pursuit of unique mental and physical states.
When Marina was asked in 2000 to create a lodging for visitors inside an old farmhouse in remote Niigata Prefecture, the
result was her "Dream House", where conceptual art collides
and merges with *tatami* and old wood. Neither Western nor
Japanese, it's a space that could only be called "Marina." Visitors read her "spiritual recipes" for dreaming, scrawled in bright
red on white signs; they sleep in "dreaming suits" color-coded
to fit the deep red, yellow, green, and purple of the "dreaming
rooms" and coffin-like "dream beds." Afterwards they record
their dreams in journals. This lodging exists because of an ele-
ment in modern Japanese design that goes far beyond esthet-
ics: experimentation. Communities in Japan are experimenting
with living spaces in surprising ways, sometimes more drasti-
cally than the West. What is very Japanese about this house is
the fact that Marina was asked to design it.

Die in Belgrad geborene Performance-Künstlerin Marina Abramovich ist dafür berühmt, bis an ihre äußersten Grenzen zu gehen. Als Marina gebeten wurde, eine Besucherunterkunft in einem alten Bauernhaus in der Präfektur Niigata zu entwerfen, entstand 2000 ihr „Dream House", wo sich Konzeptkunst mit *tatami* und altem Holz vermischt. Das Ergebnis ist weder westlich noch japanisch, sondern ein Raum, den man einfach nur mit „Marina" überschreiben kann. Besucher lesen ihre „spirituellen Traumrezepte", die in Grellrot auf weiße Schilder gekritzelt wurden. Sie schlafen in farbcodierten „Traumanzügen", passend zu den roten, gelben, grünen und lilafarbenen „Traumzimmern" und sargähnlichen „Traumbetten". Anschließend halten sie ihre Träume in Tagebüchern fest. Diese Unterkunft existiert dank der Experimentierfreude des japanischen Designs. Überall in Japan entstehen Gebäude mit lebendiger Architektur und überraschen damit immer wieder aufs Neue. Besonders „japanisch" an diesem Haus ist der Umstand, dass man Marina um dieses Experiment gebeten hat.

Née à Belgrade, l'artiste Marina Abramovich est connue pour ses performances extrêmes dans sa quête d'états mentaux et physiques hors normes. En 2000, quand on lui a demandé de créer un lieu d'hébergement dans une vieille ferme de la préfecture de Niigata, elle a créé « la maison des rêves », où l'art conceptuel se heurte et fusionne avec le *tatami* et les bois anciens. Ni occidental ni japonais, cet espace ne pouvait être inventé que par elle. On y lit ses recettes spirituelles pour rêver, écrites en rouge vif sur des panneaux blancs. On dort dans des « costumes pour rêver » assortis aux « chambres pour rêver » rouge sombre, jaunes, vertes et violettes, allongés dans des « lits pour rêver » qui ressemblent à des cercueils. Ensuite, on décrit ses songes dans des cahiers. Le design moderne japonais possède une caractéristique qui va bien au-delà de l'esthétique : l'expérimentation. Des communautés explorent sans cesse de nouveaux espaces surprenants, parfois plus radicaux qu'en Occident. Ce qu'il y a de plus japonais dans cette maison, c'est qu'on l'ait commandée à Marina.

LEFT PAGE:
Built one hundred years ago in a small village in Niigata, the farmhouse exterior remains virtually unchanged.

RIGHT PAGE:
Beyond the "telepathy telephone" is the staircase leading up to the dream rooms.

LINKE SEITE:
Das Äußere des Bauernhauses, das vor hundert Jahren in einem kleinen Dorf der Präfektur Niigata errichtet wurde, blieb so gut wie unverändert.

RECHTE SEITE:
Hinter dem „Telepathy telephone" führt eine Treppe hoch zu den Traumzimmern.

PAGE DE GAUCHE:
Construite il y a un siècle dans un petit village de Niigata, la ferme a conservé sa façade presque intacte.

PAGE DE DROITE:
Derrière le « téléphone télépathique », l'escalier qui mène aux chambres de rêve.

102

LEFT ABOVE:
The red Dream Room with coffin-like dream bed. Dream rooms come in five colors: green, blue, purple, yellow and red.

LEFT BELOW:
Custom-made dreaming suits in colors matched to the dream rooms. Each suit is fitted with magnets to transform the body into a conduit for dreaming.

RIGHT ABOVE:
On arrival, guests first enter the "Explanation Room," where 24 glasses of "power-water" are placed on top of magnets on a table.

RIGHT BELOW:
"Spiritual recipes" on the walls, hanging paper lamps, and dream journals.

LINKS OBEN:
Das rote Traumzimmer mit dem sargähnlichen Traumbett. Traumzimmer gibt es in fünf Farben – in Grün, Blau, Lila, Gelb und Rot.

LINKS UNTEN:
Handgenähte Traumanzüge, die farblich auf die Traumzimmer abgestimmt sind. Jeder Traumanzug wurde mit Magneten versehen, die den Körper in einen Traumkanal verwandeln sollen.

RECHTE SEITE OBEN:
Gleich nach ihrer Ankunft betreten die Besucher zunächst den „Explanation Room," wo auf Magnetsockeln 24 Gläser mit „Power-water" auf dem Tisch stehen.

RECHTE SEITE UNTEN:
„Spiritual recipes" an den Wänden, papierne Hängelampen und Traumtagebücher.

EN HAUT, À GAUCHE:
La chambre de rêve rouge avec son lit sarcophage. Il y a cinq couleurs de chambre : vert, bleu, violet, jaune et rouge.

EN BAS, À GAUCHE:
Des combinaisons pour rêver dans des couleurs assorties à chaque chambre. Chaque costume est équipé d'aimants pour transformer le corps en conducteur de rêve.

PAGE DE DROITE, EN HAUT:
En arrivant, les visiteurs passent d'abord par la « salle des explications » où 24 verres « d'eau de force » sont posés sur des aimants sur une table.

PAGE DE DROITE, EN BAS:
Des « recettes spirituelles » sur les murs, des lanternes en papier et des livres de rêves.

DREAM HOUSE / TOKAMACHI – NIIGATA

HOSHI ONSEN - CHOJUKAN

KUNIO OKAMURA
NIIHARU, GUNMA

The founders of the Meiji Restoration in 1868, believing that the country must Westernize to preserve its independence from European powers, banned samurai swords, and decreed that women change from kimonos to bustles. They built *Roku-meikan,* "The Deer Cry Pavilion," a dance hall where the Tokyo elite waltzed with foreign guests. While lost now, *Rokumeikan,* with its arched windows and high ceilings set the standard for "Meiji romance" architecture that was copied throughout the country. *Chojukan* bathhouse at Hoshi Onsen spa, built in 1875, is an early example of the genre, with the added twist that the "dance floor" is water. Separated by wooden logs into four large pools, hot medicinal water from a thermal vent bubbles up through pebbles underfoot. The spa stands alone in a national park deep in the mountains of Gunma Prefecture, northwest of Tokyo. The Hoshi River runs through the grounds, crossed by a covered bridge. The "garden" is the wild forest outside; inside the vestibule a fire burns in an *irori* floor-hearth, keeping guests warm during the long winter months.

A covered walkway connecting the guesthouse and bathhouse bestrides Edogawa Pond.

Eine überdachte Brücke, die das Gäste- mit dem Badehaus verbindet, führt über den Edogawa-Teich.

Un pont couvert enjambe l'étang Edogawa, reliant la pension à la maison de bains.

Die Begründer der Meiji-Restauration glaubten 1868, das Land müsse verwestlicht werden, um seine Unabhängigkeit gegenüber den europäischen Mächten zu bewahren. Sie verbannten sämtliche Samurai-Schwerter und befahlen den Frauen, Gesäßpolster statt Kimonos zu tragen. Sie errichteten das *Rokumeikan*, den „Ruf-der-Hirsche-Pavillon" – eine Unterkunft für ausländische Gäste. Obwohl das *Rokumeikan* nicht erhalten geblieben ist, wurden seine Bogenfenster und hohen Decken zum architektonischen Vorbild für das ganze Land. Das *Chojukan*-Badehaus in Hoshi Onsen von 1875 ist ein frühes Beispiel für diese Baugattung. Heißes Wasser aus einer Thermalquelle sprudelt durch die Kiesel am Boden nach oben. Das Spa liegt einsam in einem Nationalpark, tief in den Bergen der Präfektur Gunma, nordwestlich von Tokyo. Der Hoshi-Fluss fließt durch die Anlage, über den eine überdachte Brücke führt. Als „Garten" dient der wilde Wald vor der Tür. Im Vestibül wärmt eine im Boden eingelassene Feuerstelle *(irori)* die Gäste während der langen Wintermonate.

En 1868, les fondateurs de la restauration Meiji, voulant moderniser le pays pour protéger son indépendance des puissances européennes, interdirent les épées samouraïs et décrétèrent que les femmes devaient abandonner le kimono pour la crinoline. Ils bâtirent *Rokumeikan* « le pavillon du cri du cerf », une salle de bal où le gratin de Tokyo valsait avec les clients étrangers. Elle a disparu depuis mais, avec ses fenêtres en arc et ses hauts plafonds, elle donna le ton du « romantisme Meiji », une architecture imitée dans tout le pays. Construite en 1875, la *Chojukan*, dans le spa Hoshi Onsen, est un des premiers exemples du genre. Dans quatre bassins séparés par des rondins de bois, l'eau thermale bouillonne entre les galets sous vos pieds. Le spa est isolé dans un parc national au cœur des montagnes de la préfecture de Gunma, au nord-ouest de Tokyo. Un pont couvert permet d'enjamber le Hoshi qui traverse le domaine. La forêt environnante fait office de « jardin ». Dans le vestibule, un *irori*, (foyer aménagé dans le sol) réchauffe les hôtes pendant les longs mois d'hiver.

The two-story wooden
Annex (left) and women-
only Dressing Pavilion
(right), beside Hoshi River.

Der zweistöckige hölzerne
Anbau (links) und die Frau-
enumkleide (rechts) am
Hoshi-Fluss.

L'annexe en bois de deux
étages (à gauche) et le
vestiaire des femmes (à
droite) au bord du Hoshi.

110

LEFT ABOVE:
Irori (floor hearth) room. Every morning and evening guests can come and drink tea boiled over a wood fire.

LEFT BELOW:
Exterior of Hoshi-no-yu, the main bathhouse.

RIGHT ABOVE:
A bathhouse with double-tiered roof, with open-air and interior pools.

RIGHT BELOW:
View from a guest room through trees to Hoshi-no-yu bathhouse.

LINKS OBEN:
Das irori-Zimmer mit der in den Boden eingelassenen Feuerstelle. Jeden Morgen und Abend können die Gäste hier Tee trinken, der über einem Holzfeuer zubereitet wird.

LINKS UNTEN:
Die Fassade von Hoshi-no-yu, dem Hauptbadehaus.

RECHTE SEITE OBEN:
Ein Badehaus mit Doppeldach. Es verfügt über Außen- und Innenbecken.

RECHTE SEITE UNTEN:
Blick aus einem Gästezimmer. Hinter den Bäumen erkennt man das Hoshi-no-yu-Badehaus.

EN HAUT À GAUCHE:
Le irori (foyer creusé dans le sol). Le matin et le soir, les hôtes viennent boire du thé préparé au-dessus d'un feu de bois.

EN BAS À GAUCHE:
L'extérieur d'Hoshi-no-yu, la maison de bains principale.

PAGE DE DROITE, EN HAUT:
Une maison de bains au toit à deux niveaux, ouverte aux éléments et abritant des bassins intérieurs.

PAGE DE DROITE, EN BAS:
Vue d'une chambre, la maison de bains Hoshi-no-yu entre les arbres.

HOSHI ONSEN – CHOJUKAN / NIIHARU – GUNMA

The washing area of
Hoshi-no-yu, with high
arched Meiji period win-
dows.

FOLLOWING DOUBLE PAGE:
The sunken chestnut tub
is divided into eight basins
by round floating logs
which serve as headrests
while soaking in water
piped directly from the
river bed.

Der Waschbereich im
hoshi-no-yu mit großen
Bogenfenstern aus der
Meiji-Ära.

FOLGENDE DOPPELSEITE:
Schwimmende Balken un-
terteilen den in den Boden
eingelassenen Kastanien-
holzzuber in acht Becken.
Sie schwimmen in Wasser
und dienen auch als Kopf-
stütze.

La salle de toilette
d'Hoshi-no-yu, dotée de
hautes fenêtres en arc de
la période Meiji.

DOUBLE PAGE SUIVANTE:
Le grand bassin encastré
en châtaignier est divisé
en huit par des troncs flot-
tants servant de repose-
tête pendant le bain.

112

HOSHI ONSEN – CHOJUKAN / NIIHARU – GUNMA

FOREST FLOOR

BY KENGO KUMA
NAGANO

Old-style Japanese houses stand on wooden supports raised a few feet above the ground, a trace of Southeast Asian roots, when such houses stood high on pillars in the forest. Architect Kengo Kuma's Forest Floor house reinvents this tradition of translucence, fragility, and openness. With its main supporting column hidden deep under the house, the cubical superstructure appears to rest on slim tubes placed around the sides, so frail as to hardly seem capable of bearing weight. The steps and railings are so insubstantial as to almost disappear. Above this floats not so much a series of rooms as an open floor, a glassed viewing platform overlooking the woods outside. Accentuating the sense of lightness, the house is entirely white, both outside and inside, with pale wooden floors. "I want to recover the Japanese tradition, not of 'monuments', but of 'weaker' buildings." says Kuma. In this house, what is man-made is thin, fragile, white, flat, and transparent, a delicate craft afloat in a sea of verdant nature.

Fragile white steel steps lead up to a white slatted balcony.

Zierliche weiße Stahlstufen führen zu einem Balkon mit weißen Holzlamellen hinauf.

De délicates marches en acier blanc mènent au balcon protégé d'un store à lamelles.

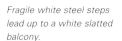

Traditionelle japanische Häuser werden auf Holzpfählen errichtet und befinden sich mehrere Zentimeter über dem Boden. Das Forest Floor House des Architekten Kengo Kuma hat diese Tradition neu interpretiert. Dabei handelt es sich um eine Tradition, die ganz stark durch Lichtdurchlässigkeit, Zerbrechlichkeit und Offenheit geprägt ist. Während der stützende Hauptpfeiler tief unter dem Haus verborgen ist, scheint der würfelförmige Aufbau einzig und allein auf rundum angeordneten, schlanken Röhren zu ruhen. Ein großer, offener Raum bietet einen herrlichen Blick in die Wälder. Um diese Leichtigkeit zu betonen, ist das Haus sowohl außen als auch innen ganz in Weiß gehalten und verfügt über helle Holzböden. „Ich möchte die japanische Tradition neu entdecken – aber nicht die der ‚Denkmäler', sondern die von ‚unscheinbareren Gebäuden'", so Kuma. In diesem Haus ist alles, was von Menschenhand geschaffen wurde, dünn, zerbrechlich, weiß, flach und durchsichtig, ein zartes Kunsthandwerk, das in einem Meer von Grün zu treiben scheint.

Les anciennes maisons japonaises sont légèrement surélevées sur des supports en bois, vestiges de leurs origines, quand elles étaient perchées sur de hauts pilotis dans la forêt. Forest Floor, bâtie par l'architecte Kengo Kuma, réinvente cette tradition. Tout est transparence, fragilité et ouverture. Son principal pilier de soutien étant caché sous la maison, la superstructure cubique paraît posée sur les minces tubes qui la bordent, si délicats qu'elle semble légère comme une plume. Les marches et les rampes minimalistes disparaissent presque. Au-dessus flotte un espace ouvert, un balcon en verre dominant les bois environnants. Pour renforcer cette impression de légèreté, la maison est peinte en blanc, au-dedans comme au-dehors, avec des parquets en bois clair. « Je veux renouer avec la tradition, pas les « monuments » mais les bâtiments plus « simples »...» explique Kuma. Dans ce vaisseau délicat flottant dans un océan de verdure, tout ce qui a été façonné par l'homme est mince, fragile, blanc, plat et transparent.

The second story seems
to float over insubstantial
steel supports.

Das erste Stockwerk
scheint auf fast imma-
teriellen Stahlrohren zu
schweben.

L'étage semble flotter
au-dessus de ses minces
supports en acier.

118

LEFT ABOVE:
The angular kitchen with chairs and glass table, topped with a skylight, continues the theme of whiteness.

LEFT BELOW:
Thick-cushioned headrest, lamp, and forest.

RIGHT ABOVE:
The white-themed living room is basically a transparent space, or "floor" for viewing the forest.

RIGHT BELOW:
A view of the forest can be had from under, as well as above, the "floor."

LINKS OBEN:
Die über Eck gebaute Küche mit von einem Oberlicht beleuchteten Stühlen und einem Glastisch führt das Thema „Weiß" fort.

LINKS UNTEN:
Weiche Daunenkissen, eine Lampe und der Wald.

RECHTE SEITE OBEN:
Der ganz in Weiß gehaltene Wohnraum wirkt beinahe transparent und dient als „Aussichtsplattform" für den Wald.

RECHTE SEITE UNTEN:
Einen Blick auf den Wald hat man sowohl unter- als auch oberhalb der „Aussichtsplattform".

EN HAUT, À GAUCHE:
La cuisine tout en angles avec des chaises et une table en verre, couronnée d'une lucarne, poursuit le thème de la blancheur.

EN BAS, À GAUCHE:
D'épais appuis-tête moelleux, une lampe et la forêt.

PAGE DE DROITE, EN HAUT:
Le salon blanc est un espace transparent, une plate-forme d'où contempler la forêt.

PAGE DE DROITE, EN BAS:
On peut aussi admirer la forêt sous la plate-forme.

FOREST FLOOR / NAGANO

Yoshihiro Takishita House

YOSHIHIRO TAKISHITA
KAMAKURA

Often the only way to save old *minka* (farmhouses) is to re-build them at a new location. Antique dealer and architect Yoshi-hiro Takishita has moved dozens of such houses to locations as far as the United States and Argentina. Among the largest *min-ka* in Japan are the multi-storied farmhouses of the Gifu area, known for their triangular roofs made from crossed timbers, called *gassho-zukuri*. In 1976, Takishita moved one of these to its present site on a hill overlooking Kamakura. Dating from the 18th century, the reconstructed house centers on a spacious wood-floored living room. The original structure reveals itself in the high ceiling and exposed beams, but at floor level, the room is furnished with a Western-style fireplace and armchairs. Other rooms feature *tatami* mats and *tokonoma* alcoves – all filled with Takishita's extensive collection of scrolls, screens, bamboo baskets, ceramics, rugs, and Chinese furniture. The uppermost rooms function as a study and library. The simple garden consists of stone steps, a low gate, and stone statues standing amongst grasses, flowers, and bamboo.

*Antique dealer-cum-
architect Takishita looks
out into the bamboo grove
in the North Garden.*

*Der Antiquitätenhändler
und Architekt Takishita
schaut auf den Bambus-
hain im Nordgarten.*

*Antiquaire et architecte,
Takishita contemple la
bambouseraie dans le
jardin du Nord.*

Oft besteht die einzige Möglichkeit, alte *minka* (Bauernhäuser) zu retten, darin, sie an anderer Stelle wieder aufzubauen.
Der Antiquitätenhändler und Architekt Yoshihiro Takishita hat
Dutzende solcher Häuser bis in die Vereinigten Staaten und
nach Argentinien verpflanzt. Zu den größten *minka* in Japan gehören die mehrstöckigen Bauernhäuser der Präfektur Gifu, die
für ihre Satteldächer aus verzahnten Balken in der so genannten
gassho-zukuri-Bauweise bekannt sind. Im Jahr 1976 versetzte
Takishita eines davon an seinen heutigen Standort auf einem
Hügel über Kamakura. Das wiederaufgebaute Haus aus dem 18.
Jahrhundert gruppiert sich um einen geräumigen Wohnraum mit
Holzdielen. Die Originalstruktur zeigt sich in der hohen Decke
mit dem offenen Gebälk, doch im Erdgeschoss gibt es einen Kamin im westlichen Stil und Armsessel. Andere Räume weisen
tatami-Matten und *tokonoma* (Alkoven) auf, die alle mit Takishi-
tas ausgedehnter Sammlung an Schriftrollen, Stellschirmen,
Bambuskörben, Keramik, Teppichen und chinesischen Möbeln
angefüllt sind. Die obersten Räume dienen als Arbeitszimmer.

Le meilleur moyen de sauver les vieilles *minka* (fermes)
est souvent de les reconstruire ailleurs. Antiquaire et architecte, Yoshihiro Takishita a déplacé des dizaines de maisons de
ce type jusqu'aux États-Unis et en Argentine. Les fermes de
plusieurs étages de la région de Gifu comptent parmi les plus
grandes du Japon. Elles sont connues pour leur toit triangulaire
en poutres croisées, ou *gassho-zukuri*. En 1976, Takishita en a
déplacé une sur une colline dominant Kamakura. Datant du 18e
siècle, elle est construite autour d'un spacieux séjour parqueté.
Les poutres apparentes et le haut plafond sont d'origine mais la
pièce du rez-de-chaussée a été équipée d'une cheminée et de
fauteuils à l'occidentale. Dans les autres pièces, tapissées de
tatamis, des *tokonoma* (alcôves) accueillent la vaste collection
de Takishita : rouleaux, paravents, paniers en bambou, cérami-
ques, tapis et meubles chinois. Le dernier étage abrite un bureau et une bibliothèque. Le jardin, simple, comporte des dalles
en pierre, un portail bas et des statues de pierre qui se dressent
parmi les hautes herbes, les fleurs et les bambous.

LEFT ABOVE:
A circular window, known as ensou, partially opened to reveal the bamboo grove in the North Garden.

LEFT BELOW:
A two-paneled Taisho (1912-1926) silk folding screen depicting farm women carrying flowers on their heads. A wooden sculpture of the Goddess of Mercy is to the left.

RIGHT ABOVE:
A single-story gate with tiled hipped roof leads to the main house. A pair of guardian gods are placed at each side of the entrance.

RIGHT BELOW:
A six-panel screen, a red andon floor lamp, and a two-panel screen with autumn grasses border the tatami mat section of the ground-floor level gallery.

LINKS OBEN:
Ein teilweise geöffnetes Rundfenster (ensou), gibt den Blick auf den Bambushain im Nordgarten frei.

LINKS UNTEN:
Ein zweiteiliger, mit Seide bespannter Wandschirm aus der Taisho-Zeit (1912–1926) zeigt Bäuerinnen, die Blumen auf ihren Köpfen tragen. Links davon eine Holzskulptur der Göttin der Barmherzigkeit.

RECHTE SEITE OBEN:
Ein eingeschossiges Tor mit einem ziegelgedeckten Walmdach führt zum Haupthaus. Gesäumt wird es von Wächterstatuen.

RECHTE SEITE UNTEN:
Ein sechsteiliger Wandschirm, eine rote Stehlampe (andon) und ein zweiteiliger Wandschirm mit Herbstgräsern umrahmen den mit Binsenmatten (tatami) ausgelegten Bereich in der Erdgeschossgalerie.

EN HAUT, À GAUCHE:
Une fenêtre ronde, ou ensou, partiellement ouverte pour révéler la bambouseraie du jardin du Nord.

EN BAS, À GAUCHE:
Un paravent en soie Taisho (1912-1926) à deux feuilles avec des paysannes portant des fleurs sur la tête. À gauche, une sculpture en bois de la déesse de la miséricorde.

PAGE DE DROITE, EN HAUT:
On accède à la maison principale par un portail surmonté d'un toit en tuiles. De chaque côté, un dieu monte la garde.

PAGE DE DROITE, EN BAS:
Un paravent à six feuilles, un lampadaire andon rouge et un paravent à deux feuilles avec des herbes d'automne délimitent la zone en tatamis de la galerie du rez-de-chaussée.

YOSHIHIRO TAKISHITA HOUSE / KAMAKURA

A six-panel screen depicting warriors in the Battle of Genpei, and a pair of six-panel screens entitled "Pine Beach" skirt the walls of the ground-floor gallery.

Ein sechsteiliger Stellschirm zeigt Krieger in der Schlacht von Gempei. Zwei weitere sechsteilige Stellschirme namens „Kiefernstrand" schmücken die Wände der Erdgeschossgalerie.

Un paravent à six feuilles représentant des guerriers lors de la bataille de Genpei et une autre paire de grands paravents intitulés « La plage des pins » cachent les murs de la galerie du rez-de-chaussée.

126

LEFT PAGE:
Reed mats tethered to the smoke-blackened timbers with rice-straw rope create a cozy reading room with built-in bookshelves and cabinets on the upper level of the West Gallery.

RIGHT PAGE:
In the West Gallery, Qing dynasty Chinese chair and dantsu carpets placed in the engawa (verandah), enclosed by sliding shoji doors.

LINKE SEITE:
In der Westgalerie im Obergeschoss bringen Schilfmatten, die mit Reisstrohseilen an die rauchgeschwärzten Balken gebunden wurden, Gemütlichkeit in das Lesezimmer mit Einbauregalen und Schränken.

RECHTE SEITE:
Auf der durch papierbespannte Türen (shoji) abgegrenzten Veranda (engawa) der Westgalerie finden sich chinesische Stühle aus der Qing-Dynastie sowie dantsu-Teppiche.

PAGE DE GAUCHE:
128 *Au niveau supérieur de la galerie ouest, des paillasses en roseaux attachées avec de la corde de paille de riz aux poutres noircies par la fumée créent une salle de lecture douillette avec des bibliothèques et des cabinets encastrés.*

PAGE DE DROITE:
Dans l'engawa (véranda) de la galerie ouest, fermée par des portes coulissantes shoji, un fauteuil chinois de la dynastie Qing et des tapis dantsu.

In the high-ceilinged sitting room of the West Gallery, a fire burns in the Western-style fireplace. The table is made from the doors of a kura store-house.

Im Wohnzimmer in der Westgalerie brennt Feuer in einem Kamin nach westlichem Vorbild. Der Tisch wurde aus den Türen eines Lagerhauses (kura) angefertigt.

Dans le haut salon de la galerie ouest, un feu brûle dans la cheminée à l'occidentale. La table a été créée avec les portes d'un entrepôt kura.

130

Yukiko Hanai Villa

BY EIZO SHIINA FOR YUKIKO HANAI
HAKONE, KANAGAWA

Asked by his client, designer Yukiko Hanai, to design a "farmhouse" in the woods, architect Eizo Shiina brought the woods inside, in the form of massive pillars, reaching over four metres high. Sliding glass doors opening out to more trees reinforce the illusion that the forest is a part of the house. Inside, underfloor heating, and a chimney vent over the central dining table create the cozy feeling of an alpine lodge. Shiina mixes two traditions in the design. The textured brick walls, cantilevered bridge, and stairways at the entrance foyer that lead upwards and downwards to reveal contrasting spaces – these pay homage to Frank Lloyd Wright. However, the woodwork inside comes from classical Japan. Shiina used the joinery of beam and post typical of Buddhist temples to create a multi-tiered supportive framework. Through the centre of the room he raised lofty pillars such as those found in the oldest Shinto shrines. The effect is to combine American modernism with an ancient Japanese sense of worship – as befits a lodge in the sacred forest.

Verandah wraps around the second floor, set off by cryptomeria sugi trees shorn of their branches to make them grow straight and tall.

Die Veranda, die um den gesamten ersten Stock läuft, ist von japanischen Sicheltannen umgeben. Ihre Zweige wurden beschnitten, um für einen geraden, kräftigen Wuchs zu sorgen.

La véranda fait tout le tour de l'étage, bordée de sugi (cèdres du Japon) élagués pour pousser plus droits et plus hauts.

Als der Architekt Eizo Shiina von seiner Kundin, der Designerin Yukiko Hanai, gebeten wurde, ein „Bauernhaus" im Wald zu entwerfen, holte er die Wälder in der Gestalt massiver, mehr als vier Meter hoher Säulen nach innen. Glasschiebetüren geben den Blick auf weitere Bäume frei und verstärken die Illusion, der Wald sei ein Teil des Hauses. Im Innern verbreiten eine Fußbodenheizung und ein Kaminabzug über dem zentral platzierten Esstisch die gemütliche Atmosphäre einer Alpenhütte. Shiinas Design verbindet zwei Traditionen: Die rauen Ziegelwände, die ausladende Brücke sowie die Treppen am Eingang zum Foyer, die nach unten und nach oben führen, sind eine Hommage an Frank Lloyd Wright, die Holzarbeiten im Innern stammen jedoch aus dem klassischen Japan. Shiina verwendete die für buddhistische Tempel typische Holzständerbauweise. In der Mitte des Raumes erheben sich große Pfeiler, wie man sie in uralten Shinto-Schreinen antrifft. Mit dem Erfolg, dass die amerikanische Moderne mit dem uralten japanischen Sinn für Stille und Andacht verbunden wird.

Quand Yukiko Hanai lui a commandé une «ferme» dans les bois, l'architecte Eizo Shiina a fait rentrer la forêt à l'intérieur sous forme de colonnes massives de quatre mètres de hauteur. Les portes coulissantes en verre qui s'ouvrent sur d'autres arbres accentuent l'illusion d'un environnement intégré dans la maison. À l'intérieur, le chauffage par le sol et la hotte de cheminée au-dessus de la table de la salle à manger créent l'atmosphère douillette d'un chalet. Shiina a combiné deux traditions. Les murs en briques texturées, le pont en console et l'escalier de l'entrée qui relie deux espaces contrastants rendent hommage à Frank Lloyd Wright. Mais, à l'intérieur, les boiseries renvoient au classicisme japonais. Shiina a utilisé une charpenterie typique des temples bouddhistes pour créer une structure de soutien de différents niveaux. Au centre de la pièce, de hauts piliers rappellent ceux que l'on voit dans les anciens sanctuaires shinto. Cette association du modernisme américain et du sens du culte du Japon ancien convient parfaitement à un pavillon situé au cœur d'une forêt sacrée.

The central room features a large table made of Japanese oak, with inset gas ranges for cooking at the table. An iron flue above the table draws smoke upwards.

Der Hauptwohnraum verfügt über einen großen Tisch aus japanischer Eiche mit eingebautem Gasherd, sodass man das Essen direkt am Tisch zubereiten kann. Eine eiserne Dunstabzugshaube beseitigt den Rauch.

Dans la pièce centrale, une grande table en chêne japonais avec des réchauds à gaz encastrés pour cuire des aliments tout en prenant ses repas. Au-dessus, une hotte en fonte.

134

YUKIKO HANAI VILLA / HAKONE – KANAGAWA

LEFT ABOVE:
Massive beams in the central room, reminiscent of temple and shrine architecture, rise to high slatted skylights. In the foreground is the wood-walled kitchen.

LEFT BELOW:
The approach: walls of textured brick overhung with branches create a passageway shutting out the outside world.

RIGHT:
With shoji doors open, the view over the central oak table with iron flue looks out through a wide glass window, topped with a wood-framed glass transom, into the forest.

LINKS OBEN:
Die massiven Balken im Hauptwohnbereich erinnern an die Tempel- und Schreinarchitektur und reichen bis zu den lamellengeschützten Oberlichtern hinauf. Im Vordergrund ist die holzvertäfelte Küche zu sehen.

LINKS UNTEN:
Die Idee: Dicke, von Zweigen überwachsene Ziegelwände bilden einen Durchgang, in dem man vollkommen von der Außenwelt abgeschirmt ist.

RECHTE SEITE:
Wegen des Panoramafensters hat man bei geöffneten Schiebetüren (shoji) vom Eichentisch unter der Dampfabzugshaube aus einen fantastischen Blick auf den Wald.

EN HAUT, À GAUCHE:
La charpenterie massive, rappelant l'architecture des temples et des sanctuaires, s'élève vers de grandes lucarnes à lattes. Au premier plan, la cuisine tout en bois.

EN BAS, À GAUCHE:
L'entrée : des murs en briques texturées envahis de branches créent un passage à l'abri du monde extérieur.

PAGE DE DROITE:
Quand on est assis à la table centrale en chêne, les portes shoji s'ouvrent sur une baie vitrée donnant sur la forêt et surmontée d'une imposte dans un cadre en bois.

136

YUKIKO HANAI VILLA / HAKONE – KANAGAWA

138

YUKIKO HANAI VILLA / HAKONE – KANAGAWA

Chizanso Villa

YOICHIRO USHIODA
KAMAKURA

The hills and beaches of Hayama, just south of Kamakura, were once Japan's "Newport Beach," boasting five hundred villas of the noble and wealthy, centred on an Imperial villa that is still in use. However, today only fifty villas remain, of which Chizanso is one of the most extensive. Issei Hatakeyama, an early 20th-century industrialist and noted tea ceremony connoisseur and collector, built Chizanso in the 1910's. The grounds contain a thatched gate and 16th-century temple, an Edo-period farmhouse, a *sukiya*-style teahouse designed by Togo Murano in the 1960's, and a white-plaster walled *kura* (storehouse), all dismantled and moved here from different sites. The present owner of Chizanso, Yoichiro Ushioda, continues to maintain the thatched roofs, which need to be redone every twenty years. Issho, Zen priest resident in the complex, looks after the moss gardens, tea room, rush hedges, and bamboo forest. Issho, who spent eighteen years teaching Zen in America, has turned Chizanso into a hermitage, a place to practice Zen meditation in quiet seclusion.

Issho, Buddhist monk and caretaker of the villa, sits in meditation.

Issho, buddhistischer Mönch und Hausverwalter, beim Meditieren.

Issho, moine bouddhiste et gardien de la villa, en pleine méditation.

Die Hügel und Strände von Hayama, südlich von Kamakura, waren früher so etwas wie Japans „Newport Beach", wo sich einst 500 Villen des Adels und Geldadels um eine kaiserliche Villa scharten. Doch es gibt nur noch 50 davon, von denen Chizanso eine der größten ist. Issei Hatakeyama, Industrieller des frühen 20. Jahrhunderts, berühmter Teezeremoniekenner und Sammler, erbaute Chizanso in den 1910er-Jahren. Auf dem Grundstück befinden sich ein strohgedecktes Tor und ein Tempel aus dem 16. Jahrhundert, ein Bauernhaus aus der Edo-Zeit, ein Teehaus im Laubenstil *(sukiya)*, das in den 1960er-Jahren von Togo Murano entworfen wurde, sowie ein weiß verputztes *kura* (Lagerhaus). Der heutige Eigentümer von Chizanso, Yoichiro Ushioda, hält die strohgedeckten Dächer weiterhin instand, die alle zwanzig Jahre erneuert werden müssen. Issho, Zenpriester und heutiger Bewohner des Gebäudekomplexes, kümmert sich um die Moosgärten, das Teezimmer, die Hecken und den Bambuswald. Issho hat Chizanso in eine Klause verwandelt – in einen Ort, an den man sich fernab der Welt Zen-Meditationen hingeben kann.

Les collines et les plages d'Hamaya, au sud de Kamakura, étaient autrefois un lieu de villégiature, avec plus de cinq cents villas bâties autour d'une résidence impériale. Il ne reste plus qu'une cinquantaine de villas, dont Chizanso est l'une des plus grandes. Issei Hatakeyama, un industriel du début du 20e siècle, grand collectionneur et fin connaisseur de la cérémonie du thé, la fit construire dans les années 1910. Le domaine abrite un portail au toit en chaume et un temple du 16e siècle, une ferme de l'époque Edo, une maison de thé de style *sukiya* conçue par Togo Murano dans les années soixante et un *kura* (entrepôt) aux murs en plâtre blanc. Le propriétaire actuel, Yoichiro Ushioda continue d'entretenir les toits en chaume, qui doivent être refaits tous les vingt ans. Issho, prêtre zen qui habite sur place, veille sur le jardin de mousses, la maison de thé, les haies en joncs et la bambouseraie. Après avoir enseigné le zen aux États-Unis pendant vingt ans, il est rentré au pays pour transformer Chizanso en ermitage, un lieu où pratiquer la méditation zen dans un isolement serein.

142

LEFT ABOVE:
Low door to the tea ceremony room, which guests must enter kneeling, a way of equalizing all participants to the same status.

LEFT BELOW:
Monk Issho stands in front of the old entrance gate.

RIGHT ABOVE:
Dating from the 16th century, the thatched entrance gate was built in Kamakura and moved to the estate in 1910.

RIGHT BELOW:
Side view of the Kannondo, or Bodhisattva Hall, originally built in the 15th century in Kamakura and later moved and reconstructed on the premises.

LINKS OBEN:
Die Tür zum Teeraum ist so niedrig, dass die Besucher nur kniend eintreten können. Auf diese Weise bekommen alle Teilnehmer denselben gesellschaftlichen Status.

LINKS UNTEN:
Der Mönch Issho vor dem alten Eingangstor.

RECHTE SEITE OBEN:
Das grasgedeckte Eingangstor aus dem 16. Jahrhundert wurde in Kamakura errichtet und 1910 auf diesem Grundstück neu aufgebaut.

RECHTE SEITE UNTEN:
Seitenansicht des Kannondo, bzw. der Bodhisattva-Halle. Auch sie wurde ursprünglich im 15. Jahrhundert in Kamakura erbaut, später abgetragen und hier wieder aufgebaut.

EN HAUT, À GAUCHE:
La porte basse menant à la salle de la cérémonie du thé, où l'on rentre à genoux pour que tous soient sur un plan d'égalité.

EN BAS, À GAUCHE:
Le moine Issho devant le vieux portail.

PAGE DE DROITE, EN HAUT:
Datant du 16ᵉ siècle, le portail au toit en chaume fut construit à Kamakura et déplacé sur la propriété en 1910.

PAGE DE DROITE, EN BAS:
Vue latérale du Kannon-do, ou salle du bodhisattva, construit au 15ᵉ siècle à Kamakura et déplacé plus tard sur la propriété.

CHIZANSO VILLA / KAMAKURA

"Walking meditation" inside the Kannon-do, or Bodhisattva Hall. Raised tatami platforms with cushions are for seated Zen meditation.

„Gehmeditation" im Kannon-do bzw. der Bodhisattva-Halle. Erhöhte tatami-Plattformen mit Kissen dienen der Zen-Meditation im Sitzen.

« Méditation ambulante » à l'intérieur du Kannon-do, ou salle du bodhisattva. Les bancs recouverts de tatamis servent à la méditation zen assise.

LEFT PAGE:
Antique box containing utensils for the tea ceremony, enveloped in a furoshiki (special cloth for wrapping and carrying).

RIGHT PAGE:
Gong and utensils for tea ceremony are placed inside the kura (storehouse) for safekeeping.

LINKE SEITE:
Antikes Kästchen, das Utensilien für die Teezeremonie enthält. Es wurde in einen furoshiki gewickelt, ein besonderes Einwickel- und Tragetuch.

RECHTE SEITE:
Im Lagerhaus (kura) werden der Gong sowie weitere Utensilien für die Teezeremonie sicher aufbewahrt.

PAGE DE GAUCHE:
Coffret ancien contenant les ustensiles de la cérémonie du thé, enveloppé dans un furoshiki (étoffe spéciale pour transporter des charges)

PAGE DE DROITE:
Gong et ustensiles de la cérémonie du thé rangés dans le kura (entrepôt).

Necessities for preparing tea include the chaki (tea caddy) and chashaku (scoop), the chasen (whisk), and chawan (tea bowl).

Utensilien zur Vorbereitung der Teezeremonie sind unter anderem chaki (Teedose), chashaku (Teeschöpfkelle), chasen (Schlagbesen) und chawan (Teeschale).

Les ustensiles indispensables à la préparation du thé incluent un chaki (boîte à thé), un chashaku (cuillère), un chasen (fouet) et un chawan (bol).

148

LOTUS HOUSE

BY KENGO KUMA FOR YOICHIRO USHIODA
KAMAKURA

In the hands of architect Kengo Kuma, wood, bamboo, glass, stone, plastic, and metal lend themselves to unexpected uses. At the Lotus House, constructed in 2005 for businessman Yoichiro Ushioda (owner of neighboring Chizanso Villa), Kuma arranged narrow travertine blocks in a lattice pattern, hanging the rectangles from a thin and almost invisible steel framework. Tho effect is a stone screen, suspended effortlessly, through which light and air pass freely. The house stands in forested mountain surroundings, with a small stream at the foot of the property. One enters from the second story, and here, as an architectural "prelude," a reflecting pool and wide deck set off one wing of the stone screen. Once inside the door, cantilevered stone steps lead downstairs to a central courtyard, flanked by more expanses of checkerboard stone, that face the lotus pond from which the house takes its name. White and unadorned inside, the complex embraces three elements: spare interior, lush green outer grounds, and the baroque barrier of a porous stone screen.

Screen of travertine blocks hangs at the boundary between house and pool.

Eine Travertinblende trennt das Haus vom Pool.

Un écran en blocs de travertin sépare la maison de la piscine.

Der Architekt Kengo Kuma verwendet Holz, Bambus, Glas, Stein, Plastik und Metall oft auf äußerst ungewöhnliche Weise. Beim Lotus House, das 2005 für den Geschäftsmann Yoichiro Ushioda erbaut wurde, dem auch die benachbarte Chizanso-Villa gehört, arrangierte Kuma schmale Travertinblöcke zu einem Schachbrettmuster, indem er die Rechtecke an einem dünnen, fast unsichtbaren Edelstahlgerüst aufhängte. Das Ergebnis ist eine fast schwerelos wirkende Steinblende. Das Haus liegt in einer bewaldeten Berglandschaft, zu Füßen des Grundstücks verläuft ein kleiner Fluss. Der Eingang befindet sich im ersten Stock, wo ein Wasserbassin sowie eine großzügige Dachterrasse einen Teil der Steinblende aufbrechen. Im Haus führen frei schwebende Steinstufen nach unten zu einem zentralen Innenhof mit schachbrettartigen Steinblenden und einem Lotusteich, der dem Haus seinen Namen gibt. Der im Innern weiß und schlicht gehaltene Gebäudekomplex vereint drei Elemente: minimales Interieur, üppiges Grün im Außenbereich und den verspielten Sichtschutz einer durchlässigen Steinblende.

Entre les mains de l'architecte Kengo Kuma, le bois, le bambou, le verre, la pierre, le plastique et le métal se découvrent des usages inattendus. Dans la maison du Lotus, construite en 2005 pour l'homme d'affaire Yoichiro Ushioda (propriétaire de la villa Chizanso voisine), Kuma a conçu un treillage en étroites dalles de travertin accrochées à un mince cadre en acier presque invisible, créant un effet de paravent en pierre qui semble flotter dans le vide, laissant filtrer la lumière et l'air. La maison se dresse sur une montagne boisée, un ruisseau gargouillant à ses pieds. On entre par le premier étage où, tel un «prélude» architectural, un bassin et une vaste terrasse mettent en valeur une face du paravent de pierre. Une fois la porte franchie, des marches flottantes en pierre descendent vers la cour centrale, flanquée de surfaces en damier qui font face au bassin de lotus auquel la maison doit son nom. Avec ses intérieurs blancs et nus, le complexe associe trois éléments : une décoration sobre, une végétation luxuriante et la barrière baroque d'un paravent en pierre poreuse.

Entry to the house, via
the first-floor rooftop, with
travertine wall reflected
in the shallow pool with
projecting moon-viewing
platform to the right.

Der Zugang zum Haus
führt über das Dach des
Erdgeschosses. Die Tra-
vertinwand spiegelt sich
im flachen Pool. Rechts
davon eine hervorstehen-
de Aussichtsplattform,
von der aus man den
Mond beobachten kann.

L'entrée de la maison se
fait par le toit du premier
étage, le mur en travertin
se reflétant dans le bas-
sin. À droite, une terrasse
pour contempler la lune.

152

LOTUS HOUSE / KAMAKURA

PREVIOUS DOUBLE PAGE:
*High glass walls and lotus
pond act as reflecting mir-
rors in the evening light.*

*Thin cantilevered steps
down to the marble-
floored open-plan living
room. The table and chairs
are from Bali. Beyond
the glass doors are the
kitchen and dining area.*

VORIGE DOPPELSEITE:
*In den hohen Panorama-
fenstern und dem Lotos-
Teich spiegelt sich das
Abendlicht.*

*Dünne, frei schwebende
Stufen führen hinab zum
nach oben hin offenen
Wohnraum mit Marmor-
boden. Der Tisch und
die Stühle stammen aus
Bali. Hinter den Glastüren
liegen Küche und Essbe-
reich.*

DOUBLE PAGE, PRÉCÉDENTE:
*Les hautes baies vitrées
et le bassin de lotus
miroitent dans la lumière
du soir.*

*De minces marches flot-
tantes descendent dans
le séjour ouvert au sol en
marbre. La table et les
chaises viennent de Bali.
Derrière les portes vitrées,
la cuisine/salle à manger.*

158

LEFT ABOVE:
Afternoon light streams over the table in the study and music room.

LEFT BELOW:
A black ceramic jar accents the white of the wall and cantilevered steps.

RIGHT:
On the second floor are an inside and an outside bath (rotenburo), bordered by a travertine screen, looking out at the hillside.

LINKS OBEN:
Das Nachmittagslicht strömt über den Tisch des Arbeits- und Musikzimmers.

LINKS UNTEN:
Ein schwarzes Keramikgefäß betont die eierschalfarbenen Wände und Stufen.

RECHTE SEITE:
Im ersten Stock gibt es ein Innen- und Außenbecken (rotenburo). Es wird von einer Travertinblende abgeschirmt und bietet einen schönen Blick auf die Hügel.

EN HAUT, À GAUCHE:
La table du bureau/salon de musique, baignée par la lumière de l'après-midi.

EN BAS, À GAUCHE:
Une jarre en céramique noire accentue le blanc du mur et de l'escalier.

PAGE DE DROITE:
Le premier étage comporte un bain intérieur et extérieur (rotenburo). L'écran en travertin s'ouvre sur une vue des collines.

LOTUS HOUSE / KAMAKURA

BAMBOO HOUSE

RIEKO KAWABE
KAMAKURA

Bamboo says, as no other material does, "Asia". Groves of bamboo dot the forests along the Pacific Rim from Indonesia, across Thailand and Vietnam, up through China, all the way to Japan. Graceful stalks and featherlike leaves of bamboo appear in ink drawings, screens, and scrolls. Growing straight and tall, bamboo has great strength because of its tubular structure with joints at regular intervals. Lightweight and rich in surface texture, it lends itself to a myriad of uses: floors, ceilings, windows, chairs and tables, trays, ladles, and hanging blinds. In Japan, with its cold winters, people rarely used bamboo for walls because it's difficult to seal from the elements. But modern construction techniques allow for new approaches. Rieko Kawabe's house in Kamakura uses bamboo of many varieties for walls (as well as floors, windows, and furnishings). Light and air pass through the arrays of bamboo stalks – a modern environment for a tea ceremony, housed in an ancient Asian thicket.

To the left of the entrance, screens of bamboo rise dramatically for two stories.

Links vom Eingang befinden sich gewaltige Bambuspaneele, die über zwei Stockwerke reichen.

À gauche de l'entrée, des écrans de bambou montent jusqu'au toit.

Bambus symbolisiert Asien wie kein anderes Material. Bambushaine durchziehen die Wälder der pazifischen Randgebiete von Indonesien, quer durch Thailand, Vietnam und China bis nach Japan. Die grazilen Stängel und fedrigen Blätter von Bambus sind auf Tuschzeichnungen, Stellschirmen und Schriftrollen allgegenwärtig. Bambus, der geradlinig wächst und sehr hoch wird, ist dank seiner hohlen Struktur äußerst stabil. Er ist leicht, hat eine lebhafte Maserung und kann für viele Zwecke eingesetzt werden – für Böden, Decken, Fenster, Stühle und Tische, Tabletts, Schöpfkellen und Hängerollos. Wegen der kalten Winter hat man Bambus in Japan nur selten für Wände verwendet, da er sich nur sehr schwer gegen die äußeren Elemente abschirmen lässt. Aber moderne Konstruktionstechniken erlauben neue Herangehensweisen. Rieko Kawabes Haus in Kamakura benutzt verschiedene Bambusarten für Wände und Böden, Fenster und Möbel. Licht und Luft können durch die Anordnungen von Bambusstängeln frei zirkulieren – eine moderne Umgebung inmitten eines alten asiatischen Gesträuchs.

Aucun matériau n'évoque plus l'Asie que le bambou. Des bambouseraies parsèment les étendues boisées qui bordent le Pacifique, de l'Indonésie au Japon en passant par la Thaïlande, le Viêt-nam et la Chine. Ses tiges gracieuses et ses feuilles délicates figurent dans les peintures à l'encre de Chine, ornant paravents et rouleaux. Droit et haut, son tronc tire sa grande résistance de sa forme tubulaire renforcée d'articulations à intervalles réguliers. Léger et présentant une surface riche en texture, il se prête à d'innombrables usages : sols, plafonds, fenêtres, sièges, tables, plateaux, louches et stores. Au Japon, où les hivers sont froids, il était peu utilisé pour les murs pour des raisons d'isolation. Mais les techniques modernes permettent de nouvelles expériences. La maison de Rieko Kawabe à Kamakura recourt au bambou pour de nombreux types de cloisons (ainsi que les sols, les fenêtres et le mobilier). L'air et la lumière filtrent à travers les arrangements de tiges, offrant un cadre moderne à la cérémonie du thé au cœur d'une végétation typiquement asiatique.

LEFT ABOVE:
Panel of narrow bamboo stalks provides a screen for privacy.

LEFT BELOW:
Red maple leaves and autumn grasses in front of a fence of horizontal bamboo.

RIGHT:
Organic materials create a severe geometry, framing the ocean view. The bamboo barrier (kekkai) is a traditional symbol saying "go no farther."

FOLLOWING DOUBLE PAGE LEFT:
Detail of calligraphic inscriptions on ancient bamboo stalks hung as an artwork over the fireplace.

FOLLOWING DOUBLE PAGE RIGHT:
Bamboo strips alternate with the textured surfaces of the stone fireplace, the roughly woven rug, and antique pottery jar.

LINKS OBEN:
Paneele aus schmalen Bambusstäben sorgen für Ungestörtheit.

LINKS UNTEN:
Rote Ahornblätter und Herbstgräser vor einem Zaun aus horizontalen Bambusstäben.

RECHTE SEITE:
Naturmaterialien erzeugen eine strenge Geometrie und sorgen für einen gerahmten Meerblick. Die Bambusbegrenzung (kekkai) ist ein traditionelles Symbol, das besagt: „Bis hierher und nicht weiter".

FOLGENDE DOPPELSEITE LINKS:
Detail einer kalligraphischen Inschrift auf alten Bambusstäben, die heute als Kaminschmuck dient.

FOLGENDE DOPPELSEITE RECHTS:
Bambusstäbe im Wechsel mit so unterschiedlichen Texturen wie der des Betonkamins, des grob gewebten Teppichs und des antiken Steinkrugs.

EN HAUT, À GAUCHE:
Un panneau en fins bambous protège des regards indiscrets.

EN BAS, À GAUCHE:
Des feuilles d'érable rouge et des herbes automnales devant la palissade en bambous horizontaux.

PAGE DE DROITE:
Des matériaux naturels créent une géométrie sévère, encadrant la vue sur l'océan. La barrière en bambou (kekkai) est un symbole traditionnel signifiant : « N'allez pas plus loin . »

DOUBLE PAGE SUIVANTE, À GAUCHE:
Détail de calligraphies sur des bambous anciens suspendus comme une œuvre d'art au-dessus de la cheminée.

DOUBLE PAGE SUIVANTE, À DROITE:
Les tiges de bambous créent une alternance avec les surfaces texturées de la cheminée en béton, du tapis en gros tissage et de la jarre ancienne.

BAMBOO HOUSE / KAMAKURA

LEFT ABOVE:
Concrete steps and walls are softened by the addition of bamboo panels.

LEFT BELOW:
Bamboo spout and drain in the lavatory.

RIGHT:
A desk, bamboo chair, and ink drawing on the wall, with three vertical bamboo stalks, and horizontal shadows of bamboo on the floor.

LINKS OBEN:
Stufen und Wände aus Beton wirken durch die Bambuspaneele gleich viel weniger kalt.

LINKS UNTEN:
Bambusrinne und Ablaufrohr im Waschraum.

RECHTE SEITE:
Ein Tisch, ein Bambusstuhl und eine Tuschzeichnung an der Wand. Dazu drei vertikal verlaufende Bambusstäbe sowie horizontale Bambusschattenmuster auf dem Boden.

EN HAUT, À GAUCHE:
Le béton des marches et des murs est adouci par les panneaux en bambou.

EN BAS, À GAUCHE:
Un bec et un tuyau d'écoulement en bambou dans les toilettes.

PAGE DE DROITE:
Un bureau, une chaise en bambou, une encre de Chine au mur et trois tiges verticales s'opposent aux ombres horizontales des bambous sur le sol.

BAMBOO HOUSE / KAMAKURA

PLASTIC HOUSE

BY KENGO KUMA FOR ROWLAND KIRISHIMA
TOKYO

Japan's modern architects' first love in the 1960's was concrete. But at the beginning of the 21st century, they fell into the arms of a new mistress: plastic. The very opposite of concrete, plastic is lightweight, thin-walled, translucent, and malleable – ideal for working with very small spaces. And even wealthy people in Tokyo today must build their homes in very small spaces. Kengo Kuma's Plastic House is an experiment in the use of FRP (fiberglass-reinforced polymer). Built for photographer Rowland Kirishima in 2002, the house, squeezed into a narrow rectangular lot, consists of two stories for Rowland and his wife, with a basement apartment for his mother. FRP forms walls, doors, and stairs, letting light filter in and through the house during the day rather like paper *shoji* doors did in houses of old. At the rear is a louvered deck that serves as a tea ceremony platform, and also as a skylight for the mother's apartment below. The boxed terrace projecting from the front of the house frames a view of Mt. Fuji.

Translucent polyurethane panels allow sunlight to filter in during the day and create a lantern-like effect at night, silhouetting the car at the entrance.

Durchsichtige Polyu-rethan-Paneele lassen tagsüber Sonne herein und sorgen nachts für einen Laterneneffekte, sodass das vor der Haus-tür geparkte Auto wie ein Schattenriss wirkt.

Les panneaux en polyuré-thane translucides laissent filtrer le soleil pendant la journée et créent un effet de lanterne la nuit, illu-minant la voiture devant l'entrée.

Die große Liebe moderner japanischer Architekten seit den 1960er-Jahren galt dem Beton. Doch zu Beginn des 21. Jahrhunderts warfen sie sich in die Arme einer neuen Geliebten – des Plastiks. Plastik ist das genaue Gegenteil von Beton: Es ist leicht, dünn, durchsichtig und verformbar – und somit ein ideales Arbeitsmaterial für extrem kleine Räume. Und in Tokyo müssen selbst äußerst wohlhabende Leute ihre Häuser auf sehr kleinen Grundstücken errichten. Kengo Kumas Plastic House ist ein einziges FRP-(fiberglasverstärktes Polymer)-Experiment. Das 2002 für den Fotografen Rowland Kirishima errichtete Haus, das sich in eine schmale, rechteckige Baulücke zwängt, besteht aus zwei Stockwerken für Rowland und seine Frau sowie einer separaten Souterrainwohnung für seine Mutter. Aus FRP sind Wände, Türen und Treppen, die tagsüber das Licht herein und von Zimmer zu Zimmer scheinen lassen – genau wie es früher die papiernen *shoji*-Türen taten. Auf der Rückseite befindet sich eine Terrasse, die als Oberlicht für die darunter liegende Wohnung der Mutter dient.

Dans les années soixante, les architectes modernes japonais sont tombés amoureux du béton. Puis, au début du 21e siècle, ils se sont découverts une nouvelle idylle : le plastique. À l'opposé du béton, celui-ci est léger, fin, translucide et malléable, idéal pour les espaces minuscules. À Tokyo aujourd'hui, même les riches vivent à l'étroit. Dans la maison en plastique, Kengo Kuma a expérimenté le FRP (polymère renforcé de fibre de verre). Construite pour le photographe Rowland Kirishima en 2002, elle est coincée sur un mince terrain rectangulaire et comporte, outre un duplex pour Rowland et sa femme, un appartement en sous-sol pour la mère de ce dernier. Le FRP permet de façonner des murs, des portes, des escaliers, tout en laissant filtrer la lumière, un peu à la manière des portes en papier *shoji* autrefois. À l'arrière, une plate-forme à claire-voie accueille la cérémonie du thé et éclaire l'appartement de la mère en contrebas. La terrasse encastrée qui saille à l'avant de la maison encadre une vue sur le mont Fuji.

PREVIOUS DOUBLE PAGE:
The kitchen and dining space of the ground floor, with glass wall and high ceiling.

LEFT ABOVE:
The ground floor living space, open to the kitchen and dining area, features an abundance of closet and cabinet space.

LEFT BELOW:
The raised louvered deck in the rear garden feeds natural light to the basement apartment below. The deck also serves as a stage for performing tea ceremonies.

RIGHT ABOVE:
Tree at the side of the tea ceremony stage. The screen of vertical plastic strips at the back gives privacy from the neighbors.

RIGHT BELOW:
The elliptic curve of the tub stands in sculptural counterpoint to the stark geometry of the house.

VORIGE DOPPELSEITE:
Der nach oben hin offene Küchen- und Essbereich mit Glaswand.

LINKE SEITE OBEN:
Das Wohnzimmer im Erdgeschoss ist zum Küchen- und Essbereich hin offen und verfügt dank der Einbauschränke über jede Menge Stauraum.

LINKE SEITE UNTEN:
Die erhöhte Bandraster- terrasse geht auf den rückwärtigen Garten hinaus und ermöglicht, dass genügend Licht in die Souterrainwohnung fällt. Hier findet auch die Teezeremonie statt.

RECHTS OBEN:
Ein Baum neben der Tee- zeremonie-Terrasse. Die vertikalen Plastiklamellen im Hintergrund schützen vor den neugierigen Blicken der Nachbarn.

RECHTS UNTEN:
Die ovale Wanne bildet einen interessanten Ge- gensatz zu der strengen Geometrie des Hauses.

DOUBLE PAGE PRÉCÉDENTE:
La haute cuisine/salle à manger du rez-de-chaus- sée, avec un mur de verre.

PAGE DE GAUCHE, EN HAUT:
Le séjour du rez-de-chaus- sée, ouvert sur la cuisine/ salle à manger, dispose de nombreux espaces de rangement.

PAGE DE GAUCHE, EN BAS:
La plate-forme en console dans le jardin arrière laisse passer la lumière dans l'appartement du dessous. Elle accueille également la cérémonie du thé.

EN HAUT, À DROITE:
Un arbre près de la plate- forme. À l'arrière, l'écran en lames de plastique verticales protège des regards des voisins.

EN BAS, À DROITE:
La vasque elliptique de la baignoire forme un contraste sculptural avec la géométrie rigoureuse de la maison.

175

PLASTIC HOUSE / TOKYO

Nakamura House

YOSHIFUMI NAKAMURA
TOKYO

When Yoshifumi Nakamura acquired his new residence, he was faced with an empty shell. With a floor 7 x 7 metres wide encircled by walls six metres high, it was a "skeleton and infill," arrangement – up to the architect to create his own space. Exceptional among contemporary architects, Nakamura's aim for his wife and himself was "comfort." To this end, he designed a two-floor dwelling with the soft colors of wood, and many a niche to relax, read a book, or lie down for a nap. Completed in 2003, Nakamura's house belongs to no identifiable style. Its appeal lies in the details. Nakamura, also a furniture designer, used the textures of many woods – chestnut and pine floors, paulownia ceilings, walnut railings, teak counters – to conjure a warm and "touchable" environment. Nakamura has created a Tokyo version of the old literati retreat of China and Japan: low-key, fitted with items of restrained but inherent quality, a place to think, read, talk with guests, and of course, to nap.

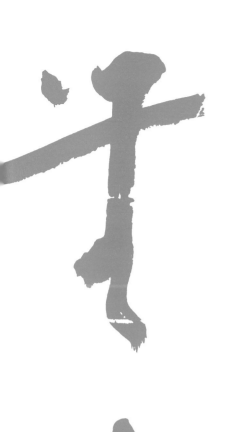

At the foot of the wooden steps up to the library, a wooden chair.

Ein Holzstuhl am Fuß der Holztreppe zur Bibliothek.

Une chaise au pied de l'escalier en bois menant à la bibliothèque.

Als Yoshifumi Nakamura sein neues Zuhause erwarb, stand er vor einer leeren Hülle. Bei den von sechs Meter hohen Wänden umgebenen 7 x 7 Metern Grundfläche handelte es sich um eine so genanntes „Skelettarrangement", sodass sein Inneres vom Architekten selbst zu gestalten war. Der herausragende zeitgenössische Architekt Nakamura wollte für sich und seine Frau vor allem eines: Behaglichkeit. Deshalb entwarf er ein zweigeschossiges Haus in verschiedenen Holzschattierungen, in denen man sich entspannen, ein Buch lesen oder ein Schläfchen machen kann. Das 2003 fertig gestellte Nakamura House ist auf keinen bestimmten Stil festgelegt. Der Reiz liegt im Detail. Nakamura, der auch Möbel entwirft, nutzte die Maserung verschiedener Hölzer – Eiche und Kiefer für die Böden, Paulownie für die Decken, Walnuss für die Geländer und Teak für die Arbeitsflächen – um eine warme, „haptische" Atmosphäre zu schaffen. Nakamura hat eine Tokyo-Version alter, chinesischer und japanischer Literatenklausen geschaffen: Unaufdringlich, mit einer schlichten, aber qualitätvollen Einrichtung.

Quand Yoshifumi Nakamura acheta sa future résidence, ce n'était qu'une coquille vide : un sol de 7 x 7 mètres entouré de murs de 6 mètres de haut. C'était un squelette sans chair. Il ne lui restait plus qu'à créer son propre espace. Fait exceptionnel pour un architecte contemporain, son mot d'ordre pour lui-même et sa femme était «confort». Il a donc conçu une habitation sur deux niveaux où dominent les tons doux du bois, remplie de recoins où se détendre, lire ou s'allonger pour une sieste. Achevée en 2003, sa maison ne relève d'aucun courant particulier. Son attrait réside dans le soin du détail. Nakamura, qui crée aussi des meubles, a utilisé les textures de nombreux bois (sols en châtaignier et pin, plafonds en paulownia, rampes en noyer, comptoirs en teck) afin de créer un environnement chaleureux et plaisant au toucher. Sa demeure est une version du Tokyo des anciennes retraites des lettrés chinois et japonais : sobre, dépouillée et ornée d'objets de qualité, un lieu où penser, lire, discuter avec des amis et, naturellement, faire la sieste.

LEFT ABOVE:
Professor Nakamura sits in the browsing alcove of his library nook, created by sliding panels over the stairwell.

LEFT BELOW:
The oval bath, rinsing buckets, upper walls, and partitioned tub cover were hand-crafted from various types of cedar.

RIGHT ABOVE:
The upper living space features a recessed black leather daybed and a 250-year-old Yi dynasty Korean vase complementing the room's spare modern lines.

RIGHT BELOW:
Professor Nakamura designed all the cabinets, tables and chairs as well as the black iron wood-burning stove.

LINKS OBEN:
Professor Nakamura in seiner Lesenische, die aus einem Schiebepaneel über der Treppe besteht

LINKS UNTEN:
Der ovale Badezuber, die Wascheimer und der obere Wandbereich sind alle handgearbeitet und bestehen aus unterschiedlichem Zedernholz.

RECHTE SEITE OBEN:
Im oberen Wohnbereich gibt es eine Einbauliege mit schwarzem Lederbezug sowie eine 250 Jahre alte koreanische Vase aus der Yi-Dynastie – ein schönes Gegengewicht zu dem ansonsten ganz modern und nüchtern gehaltenen Raum.

RECHTE SEITE UNTEN:
Professor Nakamura entwarf alle Schränke, Tische und Stühle sowie den schwarzen gusseisernen Holzofen.

EN HAUT, À GAUCHE:
Le professeur Nakamura assis dans une alcôve de sa bibliothèque, créée en faisant coulisser des panneaux sur la cage d'escalier.

EN BAS, À GAUCHE:
La baignoire, son couvercle articulé, les seaux et les boiseries hautes ont été réalisés dans différentes essences de cèdre.

PAGE DE DROITE, EN HAUT:
Dans le séjour à l'étage, un lit de repos encastré en cuir noir et un vase Yi coréen vieux de 250 ans complètent les lignes sobres et modernes de la pièce.

PAGE DE DROITE, EN BAS:
Le professeur Nakamura a dessiné tous les placards, les tables et les chaises ainsi que le poêle à bois en fonte noire.

NAKAMURA HOUSE / TOKYO

SHUTTER HOUSE
FOR A PHOTOGRAPHER

BY SHIGERU BAN, TOKYO

Shigeru Ban designs houses that change: lower the shutters and what was open to the street becomes a private space; raise them and a one-story room reveals itself as a two-story atrium. Ban admires Mies van der Rohe's "universal space," in which inside and outside flow together. When his client, a photographer, came with the request to "design like van der Rohe," Ban accepted the challenge, even though the site in the heart of Tokyo is inward looking, with a three-story house on one side and an embassy on the other. The result is the Shutter House, completed in 2003, constructed from cubical frameworks of 2 by 4 meters. Using these modules, Ban created a variety of spaces, some long, some wide, some tall, all facing internal courtyards with high trees. Raising or lowering the shutters alters the internal spaces. Old Japanese houses had a modular width between columns, and rooms that changed by sliding paper doors. Ban has re-interpreted this in modern materials, with the outside gardens brought inside. He calls it a "universal floor."

The perimeter of upper rooms facing the courtyard is lined in glass, linking inside and outside.

Die oberen Räume sind zum Innenhof hin komplett mit Glas eingefasst und sorgen so für einen nahtlosen Übergang zwischen Innen und Außen.

Dans les chambres à l'étage donnant sur la cour, des murs de verre relient l'intérieur et l'extérieur.

Shigeru Ban entwirft Häuser, die sich verwandeln lassen: Wenn man die Jalousien (engl. „shutters") herunterlässt, wird ein zur Straße hin offener Raum zum privaten Refugium. Zieht man sie hoch, entpuppt sich ein einstöckiger Raum als zweistöckiges Atrium. Ban bewundert den „kontinuierlichen Raum" eines Mies van der Rohe, bei dem Innen und Außen miteinander verschmelzen. Als ihn sein Auftraggeber, ein Fotograf, bat, ein Haus im Stil von van der Rohe zu entwerfen, nahm Ban die Herausforderung an, obwohl das mitten in Tokyo gelegene Grundstück nach hinten hinausgeht und zwischen anderen Gebäuden eingeschlossen ist. Das Ergebnis ist das Shutter House, das 2003 fertig gestellt wurde und aus mehreren würfelförmigen Modulen von zwei mal vier Metern besteht. Mit ihrer Hilfe kreierte Ban eine Vielzahl von schmal oder breit geschnittenen Räumen, die alle auf Innenhöfe mit hohen Bäumen hinausgehen. Alte japanische Häuser besaßen eine Art Baukastenarchitektur, die sich mithilfe von Schiebetüren verändern ließen. Ban hat diese Architektur mit modernen Materialien neu interpretiert.

Shigeru Ban conçoit des maisons changeantes : baissez les volets et ce qui était ouvert sur la rue devient un espace privé ; levez-les et une pièce basse devient un atrium de deux étages. Ban admire « l'espace universel » de Mies van der Rohe où l'intérieur et l'extérieur fusionnent. Quand son client, un photographe, lui commanda une maison « à la Mies van der Rohe », il releva le défi bien que le terrain, au cœur de Tokyo et coincé entre un immeuble de trois étages et une ambassade, ait plutôt invité au repli sur soi. Le résultat : Shutter House, achevée en 2003. Avec des modules de 2 x 4 mètres, Ban a créé une variété d'espaces, tantôt longs, tantôt larges, tantôt hauts, tous donnant sur des cours intérieures avec de grands arbres. En baissant ou en ouvrant les volets, on fait alterner les espaces. Les vieilles maisons japonaises possédaient une largeur modulaire entre des colonnes, les pièces changeant de forme grâce à des portes coulissantes. Ban a réinterprété cette tradition avec des matériaux modernes, les jardins extérieurs entrant à l'intérieur. Il appelle ça «le sol universel».

Expansive view of the main floor, with stacking shutters retracted under the ceiling, revealing the large and small grid modules that make up the house.

Der Hauptwohnbereich bei hochgezogenen Jalousien, sodass man die kleinen und großen Module erkennen kann, aus denen das Haus besteht.

Vue d'ensemble du rez-de-chaussée, les volets remontés sous le plafond, révélant les grands et petits modules qui composent la maison.

182

© Hiroyuki Hirai

184

© Hiroyuki Hirai

LEFT ABOVE:
The curvilinear railing and spiral staircase accentuate the rectangular-framed view of the inner courtyard.

LEFT BELOW:
Panes of clear glass and cascading greenery in a checkerboard pattern surround the central atrium.

RIGHT PAGE:
Main floor with stacking shutters lowered, creating new spatial blocks in what had been open space.

LINKS OBEN:
Die Wendeltreppe und ihr Geländer betonen den rechtwinklig angelegten Innenhof.

LINKS UNTEN:
Glaspaneele und hängende Gärten im Schachbrettmuster umgeben das Atrium.

RECHTE SEITE:
Der Hauptwohnbereich mit heruntergelassenen Jalousien. Auf diese Weise wurden aus dem einstmals offenen Raum weitere Raummodule geschaffen.

EN HAUT, À GAUCHE:
La courbe de la rampe et l'escalier en colimaçon contrastent avec le rectangle de la baie donnant sur la cour intérieure.

EN BAS, À GAUCHE:
L'atrium central est bordé d'une structure en damier où des pans vitrés alternent avec des plantes retombant en cascades.

PAGE DE DROITE:
Le rez-de-chaussée avec certains volets fermés, créant de nouvelles pièces dans ce qui était un espace ouvert.

LEFT PAGE:
The owner maintains a photography studio in the first-floor basement. A zig-zag staircase rises to the mezzanine-level workspace, and continues on to the house's upper levels.

RIGHT ABOVE:
The theme of the house is white on white, with the occasional pieces of brown or black furniture and artworks used as accents.

RIGHT BELOW:
Vines cascading down the garden wall, and tree branches stretching upwards, bring nature into the house.

LINKE SEITE:
Der Eigentümer hat sich im ersten Stock ein Foto-studio eingerichtet. Eine Zickzacktreppe führt ins Zwischengeschoss und von dort aus in die oberen Stockwerke des Hauses.

RECHTS OBEN:
Das Haus ist ganz in Weiß gehalten. Das ein oder andere Möbelstück oder Kunstobjekt in Braun oder Schwarz setzt farbliche Akzente.

RECHTS UNTEN:
Weinranken an der Gartenmauer sowie nach oben strebende Baumzweige holen Natur ins Haus.

PAGE DE GAUCHE:
Le propriétaire a installé un studio de photo au deuxième sous-sol. Un escalier en zigzag mène au bureau en mezzanine, puis continue vers les niveaux supérieurs.

EN HAUT, À DROITE:
Le thème blanc sur blanc de la maison est ponctué ici et là de la touche brune ou noire d'un meuble ou d'une œuvre d'art.

EN BAS, À DROITE:
Les plantes grimpantes sur le mur du jardin et les branches d'arbre s'élevant vers le ciel font entrer la nature dans la maison.

SHUTTER HOUSE FOR A PHOTOGRAPHER / TOKYO

Natural Strips II

BY MASAKI ENDOH FOR ICHIRO CHINO
TOKYO

Nowhere is the challenge of design for the very small house more evident than in Masaki Endoh's Natural Strips II, completed in 2005. Total floor area is 85 square meters, divided between a shop on the ground floor, living/kitchen on the second, and bedroom on the third. A pair of columns made of bent steel plate run through the middle of the house, defining the location of baths, toilets, and a small Buddhist altar. Nooks for washing machine, fax, and telephone fold away like lockers in a yacht. "People can rent books from a library," says Endoh, adding mischievously, "and although the house has a refrigerator, in the future we might not need even that, because we can buy food from a convenience store." The owners disposed of their books and most other possessions in order to live here. What they do have is light, filtering in everywhere from the walls made of twin polycarbonates, insulated with padded panels made from recycled pet bottles. At night the house glows like a lantern.

Nirgendwo wird die Herausforderung, ein sehr kleines Haus zu entwerfen, deutlicher als in Masaki Endohs Natural Strips II, das 2005 fertig gestellt wurde. Die gesamte Wohnfläche beträgt 85 Quadratmeter und gliedert sich in einen Laden im Erdgeschoss, einen Wohnraum mit Küche im ersten und ein Schlafzimmer im zweiten Stock. Ein Säulenpaar aus gebogenem Blechstahl verläuft durch die Hausmitte und teilt Bereiche für Bäder, Toiletten und einen kleinen buddhistischen Altar ab. Stauraum für Waschmaschine, Fax und Telefon verbirgt sich hinter Schiebewänden. „Die Leute können sich Bücher aus der Bücherei leihen", sagt Endoh und fügt verschmitzt hinzu: „Obwohl es im Haus einen Kühlschrank gibt, dürfte dieser in Zukunft überflüssig werden, da man seine Lebensmittel auch von einem rund um die Uhr geöffneten Supermarkt beziehen kann." Die Bewohner trennten sich von ihren Büchern und anderem Besitz, um hier leben zu können. Dafür haben sie Licht im Überfluss, das von überallher durch die Polycarbonatwände scheint. Nachts leuchtet das Haus wie eine Laterne.

Natural Strips II, achevée par Masaki Endoh en 2005, est l'illustration même du pari réussi pour construire sur un petit espace. La surface au sol est de 85m², divisée entre une boutique au rez-de-chaussée, un séjour/cuisine au premier étage et une chambre au second. Deux colonnes en plaques d'acier incurvées traversent le centre de la structure, accueillant la salle de bains, les toilettes et un petit autel bouddhiste. La machine à laver, le fax et le téléphone s'escamotent dans des trappes comme sur un yacht. Espiègle, Endoh explique: « Les livres, on peut les louer dans une bibliothèque. La maison possède un réfrigérateur mais, à l'avenir, on pourra s'en passer, commandant tous nos repas à l'extérieur. » Pour habiter la maison, les propriétaires ont dû abandonner la plupart de leurs objets familiers. En revanche, ils ont de la lumière en abondance car elle filtre partout à travers les murs en double épaisseur de polycarbonate, isolés à l'aide de panneaux matelassés réalisés avec des mini bouteilles recyclées. La nuit, la maison luit comme une lanterne.

LEFT ABOVE:
Columns shaped like crescent moons, made of bent steel plates, support the house and also divide the floors into front and back.

LEFT BELOW:
On one of the central columns is a shelf with a miniature Buddhist altar. Sliding panels, made from twin polycarbonates, encircle the house, admitting light and also insulating.

RIGHT ABOVE:
Airy third-floor bedroom. Behind the bedding is the bathroom area, framed by glass on one side, and the curving walls of the central columns.

RIGHT BELOW:
Kitchen on the second floor. Sliding panels behind the counter hide storage spaces.

LINKS OBEN:
Halbmondförmige Säulen aus gebogenen Stahlplatten stützen und unterteilen das Haus.

LINKS UNTEN:
Eine der zentralen Säulen ist gleichzeitig Regal, das einen winzigen buddhistischen Altar enthält. Schiebewände aus Polycarbonat umhüllen das Haus. Sie lassen Licht durch und dienen gleichzeitig der Isolation.

RECHTE SEITE OBEN:
Das luftige Schlafzimmer im zweiten Stock. Hinter dem Bett befindet sich der Badezimmerbereich, der auf einer Seite durch Glas und auf der anderen durch die gebogene Säule begrenzt wird.

RECHTE SEITE UNTEN:
Die Küche im ersten Stock. Die Schiebewände hinter der Arbeitsfläche verbergen weiteren Stauraum.

EN HAUT, À GAUCHE:
Des colonnes en croissants de lune, constituées de plaques d'acier incurvées, soutiennent la maison et divisent les étages.

EN BAS, À GAUCHE:
Un autel bouddhiste miniature sur une étagère sur l'une des colonnes centrales. Des panneaux coulissants en double couche de polycarbonate ceignent la maison, laissant filtrer la lumière et servant d'isolant.

PAGE DE DROITE, EN HAUT:
Une chambre claire au deuxième étage. Derrière le lit, la salle de bains avec, d'un côté, des murs en verre, de l'autre les parois arrondies des colonnes centrales.

PAGE DE DROITE, EN BAS:
La cuisine au premier étage. Des panneaux coulissants derrière le plan de travail cachent des espaces de rangement.

190

NATURAL STRIPS II / TOKYO

Glossary / Glossar / Glossaire

AJI-ISHI: High-quality granite from Aji in northern Shikoku Island, bordering on Mure. The area is famous for its high-quality gravestones made from the stone.

Hochwertiger Granit aus Aji im Norden der Insel Shikoku an der Grenze zu Mure. Die Gegend ist berühmt für ihre hochwertigen Grabsteine aus genau diesem Stein.

Beau granit provenant d'Aji au nord de l'île Shikoku, près de Mure. La région est célèbre pour ses pierres tombales de grande qualité.

AKARI: Paper lanterns designed by Isamu Noguchi, most famous for his large-scale stone sculptures.

Papierlaternen, die vom Künstler Isamu Noguchi entworfen wurden, der für seine großformatigen Steinskulpturen berühmt ist

Lanternes en papier créées par Isamu Noguchi, plus connu pour ses sculptures monumentales en pierre.

ANDON: Paper-covered lamps, noted for their suffused lighting and variant designs. The two most common forms: *kaku-andon*, a square frame raised on two legs, and *maru-andon*, a cylindrical frame.

Papierbespannte Lampen in verschiedenen Formen. Am meisten verbreitet sind *kaku-andon*, ein quadratisches Gestell auf zwei Beinen, sowie *maru-andon*, ein zylindrisches Gestell.

Lampes en papier aux formes variées diffusant une lumière tamisée. Les deux versions les plus répandues sont le kaku-andon, un carré monté sur deux pieds, et le maru-andon, cylindrique.

BIZEN-WARE: Unglazed stoneware made in the town of Imbe (in the area formerly known as Bizen), Okayama Prefecture, since the 12th century.

Unglasierte Keramik aus der Stadt Imbe (in einem Gebiet, das früher Bizen hieß), Präfektur Okayama, seit dem 12. Jahrhundert.

Pots en grès brut fabriqués dans la ville d'Imbe (autrefois Bizen) dans la préfecture d'Okayama, depuis le 12ᵉ siècle.

BUNRAKU: Traditional puppet theatre, established in 1684 in Osaka, accompanied by distinctive chanting (*joruri*) and samisen.

Traditionelles Puppentheater. Entstand 1684 in Osaka und wird von *joruri*, Rezitationen und der japanischen Laute Shamisen begleitet.

Théâtre de marionnettes traditionnel, établi en 1684 à Osaka, s'accompagnant de chants caractéristiques (joruri) et de samisen.

BYOBU: Folding screens, decorated with painting or calligraphy, which are used as room partitions, with two, four, six, or eight painted panels.

Stellschirm oder Paravent, der mit einem Gemälde oder Kalligraphien verziert ist und als Raumteiler verwendet wird. Es gibt zwei-, vier-, sechs- oder achtteilige Stellschirme.

Paravents à deux, quatre, six ou huit feuilles, décorés de peintures ou de calligraphies et servant à cloisonner des pièces.

CHAKI: A tea caddy for storing powdered green tea, often made of lacquered wood.

Teedose, in der pulverisierter grüner Tee aufbewahrt wird, häufig aus lackiertem Holz.

Coffret pour conserver le thé vert en poudre, souvent en bois laqué.

CHASEN: A tea whisk made from a piece of bamboo, one end of which is split finely into a number of thin strips. It is used to whip powdered green tea and hot water in a tea bowl until it froths.

Ein Schlagbesen aus Bambus, der an einem Ende in lauter feine Bambusspreißel ausläuft. Er wird dazu verwendet, den pulverisierten grünen Tee in einer Teeschale mit heißem Wasser zu verrühren, bis er schäumt.

Fouet réalisé en bambou dont une extrémité est fendue en fines lamelles, servant à battre la poudre de thé vert dans un bol d'eau chaude jusqu'à la faire mousser.

CHASHAKU: A tea scoop. A spoon-like utensil used to transfer powdered tea from the *chaki* to the tea bowl.

Ein Teeportionierer. Mit dem löffelähnlichen Utensil gibt man den pulverisierten Tee aus dem *chaki* in die Teeschale.

Cuillère servant à verser le thé en poudre du chaki dans le bol à thé.

CHAWAN: A ceramic bowl used in tea ceremonies, highly prized by art collectors and tea ceremony practitioners.

Eine Keramikschale für die Teezeremonie, die von Kunstsammlern und Liebhabern der Teezeremonie hoch geschätzt wird.

Bol en céramique servant à la cérémonie du thé, très recherché des collectionneurs et de ceux qui pratiquent le rite.

Glossary / Glossar / Glossaire

DANTSU: Originally from China, Turkey and the Near and Middle East, these hand-woven carpets are known for their distinctive patterns and rich colors.

Handgewebte Teppiche, die ursprünglich aus China, der Türkei, dem Nahen und Mittleren Osten stammen und für ihre unverwechselbaren Muster und Farben berühmt sind.

Initialement produits en Chine, en Turquie, au Proche et Moyen-Orient, ces tapis tissés à la main sont célèbres pour leur motifs caractéristiques et leurs couleurs riches.

DOMA: A floor of pounded or packed earth, associated with the kitchen and entrances in daily use. The *doma* usually contained the clay range, *kamado*, for cooking.

Ein Boden aus festgestampfter Erde, der mit dem täglich genutzten Küchen- und Eingangsbereich assoziiert wird. Der *doma* enthielt üblicherweise einen Lehmofen (*kamado*) zum Kochen.

Sol en terre battue ou tassée, généralement dans la cuisine et les pièces de service. Il accueillait autrefois des fours en argile ou kamado.

ENGAWA: A narrow wooden deck at the edge of a *tatami* room, similar to the Western porch or verandah. With a roof on top, it can be completely open at the sides, or fitted with sliding doors.

Eine schmale Holzterrasse vor einem *tatami*-Zimmer, die an eine westliche Veranda oder einen Balkon erinnert. Sie kann überdacht, offen oder mit Schiebetüren versehen sein.

Étroite plate-forme en bois bordant les pièces tapissées de tatamis, similaire au porche ou à la véranda en Occident. Surmonté d'un toit, il peut être ouvert ou équipé de portes coulissantes.

ENSOU: A circular window.

Ein Rundfenster.

Fenêtre ronde.

FUROSHIKI: Literally a "cloth for the bath." It is a square piece of cloth originally used during the Edo period (1603-1868) for wrapping bathing articles. Today it is used to carry or wrap all kinds of items.

Das „Badetuch" ist ein quadratisches Stück Stoff, das während der Edo-Zeit (1603–1868) ursprünglich zum Einwickeln von Badeutensilien verwendet wurde. Heute wird es zum Einwickeln und Tragen von allen möglichen Gegenständen benutzt.

Littéralement, « tissu pour le bain ». Carré d'étoffe utilisé pendant la période Edo (1603-1868) pour envelopper les articles de bain. Aujourd'hui, on l'utilise pour envelopper et transporter toutes sortes d'objets.

FUSUMA: An opaque sliding door, as distinct from *shoji* (translucent paper doors), covered with thick paper, silk or other kinds of cloth. They often serve as a surface for painting or calligraphy.

Eine Schiebetür, die im Unterschied zu *shoji*, der transparenten Papiertür, undurchsichtig ist. Sie ist mit dickem Papier, Seide oder anderen Stoffen bespannt und dient häufig auch als Untergrund für Gemälde oder Kalligraphien.

Porte coulissante opaque en papier épais, en soie ou dans un autre type de tissu, se distinguant du shoji (en papier translucide). On l'utilise souvent comme support pour la peinture et la calligraphie.

GASSHO-ZUKURI: Literally, "clasped hands." A triangular roof made from crossed timbers, called *gassho* because it resembles hands clasped in prayer.

Wortwörtlich „verschränkte Hände". Ein Satteldach aus verzahnten Balken namens *gassho*, das an betende Hände erinnert.

Littéralement « mains jointes ». Toit triangulaire en poutres croisées, évoquant les mains jointes dans la prière.

GENKAN: The entrance gallery or porch of a home or the main hall of a temple. *Genkan* often feature a tiled or earthen floor at the doorway, with a low broad plank or flat stone, where visitors remove their shoes, before stepping up into the entry hall proper.

Der Eingangsbereich eines Hauses bzw. die Haupthalle eines Tempels. *Genkan* sind häufig gefliest oder haben einen Boden aus festgestampfter Erde. Auf dem Boden befindet sich eine niedrige, breite Holzplanke oder ein flacher Stein, wo Besucher ihre Schuhe ausziehen, bevor sie den eigentlichen Hausflur betreten.

Galerie d'entrée ou porche d'une maison ou la salle principale d'un temple. Souvent précédé d'un seuil carrelé ou en terre battue équipé d'une planche large ou d'une dalle plate pour enlever ses chaussures avant d'entrer.

GETA: Traditional footwear with a flat wood sole and a "V" style toe thong, raised up on two wooden strips.

Traditionelles Schuhwerk mit V-förmigen Zehenriemen und einer flachen Holzsohle auf zwei Holzleisten.

Soulier traditionnel monté sur deux lames de bois avec une semelle plate en bois et une lanière en V.

Glossary / Glossar / Glossaire

HAIDEN:

A worship hall at a Shinto shrine, usually placed directly in front of the main sanctuary. Often it is the site for performances and offerings.

Anbetungshalle in einem Shinto-Schrein, die normalerweise direkt vor dem Haupttheiligtum liegt. Dort werden auch Rituale vollzogen und Opfergaben dargebracht.

Salle de culte dans un temple shinto, généralement placée juste devant le sanctuaire principal. Accueille souvent les cérémonies et les offrandes.

HAKO-HIBACHI:

The *hibachi*, literally "fire bowl", is a charcoal-burning brazier which serves as a source of heat. *Hako* ("box") refers to the square shape.

Hibachi, wortwörtlich „Feuerschale", ist ein Kohlebecken, das als Heizquelle dient. *Hako* („Kiste") bezieht sich auf seine rechteckige Form.

L'hibachi (« bol de feu ») est un brasero servant de source de chaleur. Hako (« boîte ») renvoie à sa forme carrée.

HINOKI:

Cypress, a highly prized light-colored wood with a straight grain.

Japanische Zypresse, ein hochwertiges, helles Holz mit einer gleichmäßigen Maserung.

Cyprès, un bois clair à grain régulier très apprécié.

HONDEN:

The main sanctuary of a Shinto shrine, which houses the *shintai*, or object containing the spiritual essence of the deity.

Das Haupttheiligtum eines Shinto-Schreins, das den so genannten Gottkörper (*shintai*) enthält.

Sanctuaire principal dans un temple shinto, abritant le shintai, ou objet contenant l'essence spirituelle de la divinité.

INUYARAI:

Curved barriers about 60 cm high made of bent strips of bamboo, used to protect the lower parts of buildings and walls from dirt or damage.

Gewölbte, etwa 60 cm hohe Barrieren aus Bambusstreifen, die an untere Gebäudeteile und Wände gelehnt werden, um sie vor Schmutz oder Beschädigungen zu schützen.

Barrières incurvées d'environ 60 cm de haut en bambou, servant à protéger le bas des bâtiments et des murs de la boue et des coups.

IRORI:

An open hearth set in the floor, that provides heat and a place for cooking or for making tea. In farmhouses, it was the focus of everyday life.

Eine offene, in den Boden eingelassene Feuerstelle, die Wärme spendet, aber auf der auch Mahlzeiten und Tee zubereitet werden. In Bauernhäusern bildeten sie den Lebensmittelpunkt.

Foyer ouvert aménagé dans le sol, servant à chauffer, cuisiner et préparer le thé. À la campagne, il était le centre de la vie quotidienne.

ISHI-DORO:

Stone lanterns (also called *toro*) were first used as offerings at temples and shrines. Since the 16th century they have been used in tea ceremony gardens, and today they are a common feature in gardens everywhere.

Steinlaternen (auch *toro* genannt) dienten ursprünglich als Opfergaben für Tempel und Schreine. Vom 16. Jahrhundert an wurden sie auch in Teegärten verwendet. Heute gehören sie zur ganz normalen Gartenausstattung.

Lanternes en pierre (également appelées toro) autrefois présentées en offrandes dans les temples et les sanctuaires. À partir du 16e siècle, placées dans les jardins de cérémonie du thé. Aujourd'hui, on en trouve dans tous les jardins.

JODAN:

A part of the floor in aristocratic homes that was elevated a step higher, reserved for people of high rank. Today it is often an extension of the *tokonoma* alcove with shelves bearing artworks.

Leicht erhöhter Bodenbereich in Adelspalästen, der für ranghöhere Personen reserviert war. Heute dient er häufig als Ziernische und enthält Regale mit Kunstwerken.

Partie du sol surélevée dans les demeures de l'aristocratie, réservée aux personnes de haut rang. Aujourd'hui, elle forme souvent une extension d'alcôve tokonoma, agrémentée d'étagères pour accueillir des œuvres d'art.

KAWARA:

Roof tiles made of fired clay introduced to Japan from Korea during the 6th century along with Buddhism.

Dachziegel aus gebranntem Ton, die ursprünglich aus Korea stammen und im 6. Jahrhundert mit dem Buddhismus nach Japan gelangten.

Tuiles en argile cuite provenant de Corée et introduites au Japon au 6e siècle avec le bouddhisme.

KAYA:

Thatching material, consisting of cut *susuki* grass, often translated as miscanthus reed.

Susuki-Gras zum Dachdecken, das häufig mit Miscanthus übersetzt wird.

Herbes susuki coupées, souvent appelées miscanthus ou roseau de Chine, pour faire les toits en chaume.

Glossary / Glossar / Glossaire

KEKKAI:
Symbolic barrier indicating that one should proceed no further.

Symbolische Begrenzung, die besagt: Bis hierher und nicht weiter.

Barrière symbolique indiquant qu'on ne doit pas aller au-delà.

KURA:
A thick-walled fireproof storehouse in which to keep valuables. The wooden frame is covered by mud and then finished with a coat of plaster.

Ein dickwandiges, feuersicheres Lagerhaus zur Aufbewahrung von Wertgegenständen. Sein Holzgerüst wurde erst mit Lehm und dann mit Gips verputzt.

Entrepôt aux murs épais résistants au feu pour stocker des biens de valeur. La structure en bois est couverte de boue puis enduite d'une couche de plâtre.

MACHIYA:
A merchant town house. Typically the house faced the public street, and combined a family home with a workshop, office, or retail space which was usually at the front of the house.

Das Stadthaus eines Kaufmanns, das normalerweise von der Straße aus betreten werden kann. Das Haus enthielt Wohn- und Geschäftsräume, Letztere auf der Hausvorderseite.

Maison de ville d'un marchand. Donnant généralement sur la rue et associant une résidence à un atelier, un bureau ou une boutique, le plus souvent situés à l'avant de la maison.

MARUMADO:
A circular window of which there are many varieties: some with *shoji* paper sliding doors, with patterned lattices, and others of glass.

Ein Rundfenster, von dem es viele Variationen gibt: Manche verfügen über papierne, andere über gläserne Schiebetüren.

Fenêtre ronde pouvant revêtir différentes formes : équipée de portes coulissantes shoji, d'un treillis à motifs ou d'une vitre.

MINKA:
A general term for traditional rural homes

Überbegriff für traditionelle, ländliche Wohnbauten.

Terme général pour les maisons traditionnelles à la campagne.

MISU:
A form of *sudare* (bamboo blinds) used in shrines, palaces, and aristocratic residences.

Eine *sudare*-Variante, die für Schreine, Paläste und Adelswohnsitze verwendet wird.

Forme de sudare (store en bambou) utilisé dans les temples, les palais et les résidences aristocratiques.

MUSHIKO-MADO:
A slatted window, often cut out of a plaster wall in the upper part of a building, to illuminate rooms or lofts.

Fensterschlitze im Obergeschoss eines Hauses.

Fenêtre en lamelles, souvent percée dans un mur en plâtre, à l'étage d'un bâtiment pour laisser passer la lumière dans les pièces ou le grenier.

MUSHIRO:
Roughly woven straw mats for sitting, usually around an *irori* floor hearth.

Grob gewebte Strohmatten zum Sitzen, die normalerweise um eine in den Boden eingelassene Feuerstelle (*irori*) gruppiert werden.

Paillasses grossièrement tissées, généralement placées autour d'un irori.

NABESHIMA:
Hand-woven rugs in Chinese style from Nabeshima fief in Kyushu.

Handgewebte Teppiche im chinesischen Stil aus Nabeshima in Kyushu.

Tapis tissés à la main dans le style chinois provenant du fief Nabeshima à Kyushu.

NOREN:
A banner hanging at entrances of a building, or doorways to kitchens and workshops. Two or more strips of material are sewn together at the top only, making it easy to walk through.

Ein Stoffvorhang vor Eingängen bzw. Durchgängen zur Küche oder zu Arbeitsräumen. Zwei Stoffstreifen werden nur oben zusammengenäht, damit man leichter hindurchgehen kann.

Bannière suspendue à l'entrée d'un bâtiment ou devant la porte des cuisines et des ateliers. Constituée de plusieurs bandes de tissu cousues au sommet pour faciliter le passage.

ONSEN:
Natural volcanic hot spring spa. Basically a public bath with accommodations (that may be very luxurious), *onsen* are popular vacation retreats.

Heißes, vulkanisches Quellbad. Meist handelt es sich dabei um ein öffentliches Bad mit angeschlossenen Räumlichkeiten, die sehr luxuriös sein können. *Onsen* sind beliebte Ferienziele.

Sources chaudes naturelles d'origine volcanique. Bains publics avec hébergement (parfois très luxueux), lieux de villégiature très prisés.

Glossary / Glossar / Glossaire

ROTENBURO:	Outdoor bath in *onsen*.	Außenbecken in *onsen*.	Bain extérieur dans un onsen.
RYOKAN:	Inns where guests stay in traditional interiors following Japan's old life-style: *tatami*-matted rooms, futon mattresses, *yukata*, (cotton kimonos), and hot baths.	Gästehäuser mit traditioneller Einrichtung, in denen der altjapanische Lebensstil gepflegt wird: Es gibt mit Binsenmatten (*tatami*) ausgelegte Zimmer, Futons, *yukata* (Baumwollkimonos) und heiße Bäder.	Auberge au décor traditionnel reflétant l'ancien art de vivre japonais, avec des tatamis, des futons, des yukata (kimonos en coton) et des bains chauds.
SHOIN:	A style used for aristocratic mansions in the Momoyama Period (1574-1603), and further developed in later eras, characterized by a decorative alcove or *tokonoma*.	Ein Baustil für Adelssitze während der Momoyama-Periode (1574–1603), der in späteren Epochen weiterentwickelt wurde und durch eine Ziernische (*tokonoma*) gekennzeichnet ist.	Style décoratif des demeures aristocratiques de la période Momoyama (1574-1603) puis peaufiné au fil des siècles, caractérisé par des alcôves tokonoma.
SHOJI:	Wooden-framed sliding doors covered with translucent paper on one side of the frame.	Schiebetüren, deren Holzgerüst auf einer Seite mit transparentem Papier bespannt ist.	Portes coulissantes en papier translucide avec un cadre en bois.
SOBA:	Buckwheat. Used for a variety of purposes, including a spaghetti-like noodle.	Buchweizen. Er wird vielseitig eingesetzt, zur Herstellung von spaghettiartigen Nudeln.	Blé noir, préparé de nombreuses manières, y compris pour faire des sortes de spaghettis.
SUDARE:	Blinds made of thinly shaved strips of bamboo threaded together, sometimes bordered with silk or brocade. In the summertime they are hung outside to screen out the rays of the sun.	Rollos aus dünnen, zusammengebundenen Bambusstreifen, die manchmal mit Seide oder Brokat eingefasst sind. Im Sommer werden sie rausgehängt, um das Sonnenlicht abzuschirmen.	Stores en fins éclats de bambou tressés, parfois bordés de soie ou de brocart. L'été, ils sont suspendus à l'extérieur pour filtrer le soleil.
SUGI:	Cryptomeria, a member of the cypress family. It grows tall and straight and very old trees soar as high as 70 metres.	Japanische Sicheltanne, eine Pflanze aus der Zypressenfamilie, von besonders hohem und aufrechtem Wuchs. Sehr alte Bäume können bis zu 70 Meter hoch werden.	Cryptomère, ou cèdre du Japon. Poussent hauts et droits, les plus âgés pouvant atteindre 70 mètres.
SUKIYA:	A style of fanciful and lightweight tea-influenced construction that extended to home architecture.	Ein von Teeblättern inspirierter, verspielter, leichtgewichtiger Architekturstil.	Style architectural raffiné et léger initialement destiné aux chambres à thé et qui s'est étendu ensuite à l'ensemble des maisons.
SUZURI-BAKO:	Box for keeping ink, brush, and inkstone. *Suzuri* refers to the inkstone used for grinding *sumi* (charcoal) ink sticks.	Kästchen zur Aufbewahrung von Tusche, Pinseln und Tuschestein. Der Begriff Suzuri bezieht sich auf den Tuschestein zum Reiben von *sumi* (Holzkohletuschestäbe).	Coffret pour ranger l'encre, la brosse et la pierre à encrer. Suzuri renvoie à la pierre utilisée pour broyer les bâtonnets d'encre sumi (charbon de bois).
TAMBA-WARE:	Lightly glazed or unglazed stoneware pottery from the Tamba region, west of Kyoto. *Tamba-ware* is typically used for storage jars and vases.	Dünn glasierte oder unglasierte Steingutkeramik aus der Region Tamba, westlich von Kyoto. Krüge und Vasen sind häufig aus Tamba-Keramik.	Poterie en grès légèrement vernie ou laissée brute, provenant de la région de Tamba à l'ouest de Kyoto. Généralement utilisée pour les jarres et les vases.

Glossary / Glossar / Glossaire

TATAMI: A mat, roughly 3 cm thick, with a smooth surface made of tightly woven *igusa* grass over a base of straw. Sides are usually bound with dark cloth, but in luxurious settings the binding may be made of brocade. Today, *tatami* mats are laid over the entire floor area. *Tatami* have standardized sizes, and the short side always measures half the length of the long side. *Tatami* have had a great impact on the modularity of traditional architecture.

Eine ungefähr 3 cm dicke Matte mit glatter Oberfläche aus eng gewobenem *igusa*-Gras mit Strohfüllung. Die Kanten sind meist mit einem dunklen Stoff eingefasst, aber in einem luxuriösen Ambiente sieht man sie auch mit Brokateinfassungen. Heute wird der gesamte Boden mit *tatami* ausgelegt. *Tatami* haben Standardgrößen, die Breitseite misst jeweils exakt die Hälfte der Längsseite. *Tatami* hatten einen großen Einfluss auf das Baukastenprinzip der traditionellen Architektur.

Matelas d'environ 3 cm d'épaisseur avec une surface lisse en herbes igusa finement tressées sur une base en paille. Les bords sont généralement cousus d'un tissu sombre mais les plus luxueux sont en brocart. Aujourd'hui, les tatamis tapissent la totalité du sol ; leur taille est standardisée, la largeur faisant la moitié de la longueur. Ils ont joué un rôle crucial dans la composition modulaire de l'architecture traditionnelle.

TETSUBIN: Iron teapot, derived from Chinese *sencha*, a form of tea ceremony that uses tea leaves instead of powdered tea.

Gusseiserne Teekanne, die aus der chinesischen *sencha*-Teezeremonie übernommen wurde, bei man Teeblätter statt pulverisierten Tee verwendet.

Théière en fonte inspirée du sencha chinois, forme de cérémonie du thé où celui-ci est utilisé en feuilles plutôt qu'en poudre.

TOKONOMA: A small alcove raised above the level of the floor. Originally used as the seat for a guest of high rank, it became a place to display artworks such as hanging scrolls.

Eine schmale Nische über Bodenniveau, die ursprünglich höherrangigen Personen als Sitzgelegenheit diente. Anschließend wurde sie zur Ziernische, in denen man Kunstwerke wie Schriftrollen aufhängte.

Petite alcôve surélevée. Autrefois destinée à asseoir les invités de marque, elle sert aujourd'hui à exposer des œuvres d'art telles que des rouleaux.

TSUBONIWA: Literally "garden in a jar," referring to small inner courtyard gardens.

Wortwörtlich ein „Flaschengarten", gemeint sind kleinen Innengärten.

« Jardin en bouteille » ; désignant les petits jardins intérieurs.

TSUKUBAI: Literally "stooping basin," so named because one has to stoop down to use it. A purification basin in a tea garden used for rinsing the hands and mouth before entering a tea ceremony room.

Wortwörtlich „Bückbecken," weil man sich bücken muss, um es zu benutzen. Ein Becken im Teegarten, an dem man sich Hände und Mund wäscht, bevor man den Teeraum betritt.

Littéralement « bassin où l'on se courbe » car il faut se pencher pour l'utiliser. Bassin de purification dans un jardin de thé, servant à se laver les mains et se rincer la bouche avant d'entrer dans la salle de cérémonie.

YUKIMI-SHOJI: Literally "snow-viewing *shoji*." A *shoji* door which has a lower piece that slides away, or is simply cut out, to reveal the view beyond. The open lower portion is usually glassed.

Wortwörtlich „Schneebetrachtungs-*shoji*." Eine papierbezogene Schiebetür (*shoji*) mit einer meist verglasten Aussparung, die es erlaubt, die Aussicht dahinter zu genießen.

« Shoji pour voir la neige ». Porte shoji en papier dont la partie inférieure est coulissante, vitrée ou simplement ouverte pour révéler la vue de l'autre côté.

ZASHIKI: A *tatami*-matted reception room reserved for guests, usually featuring a *tokonoma* alcove.

Ein mit *tatami* ausgelegter Empfangsraum für Besucher, der normalerweise eine Ziernische (*tokonoma*) enthält.

Salle de réception tapissée de tatamis réservée aux invités, comportant généralement une alcôve tokonoma.

Addresses / Adressen / Adresses

ARCHITECTS

TADAO ANDO ARCHITECT & ASSOCIATES
5-23-2 Toyosaki
Kita-ku, Osaka 531-0072
PHONE: +81 6 6375 1148
FAX: +81 6 6374 6240

SHIGERU BAN ARCHITECTS
5-2-4 Matsubara
Setagaya-ku, Tokyo 156-0043
PHONE: +81 3 3324 6760
FAX: +81 3 3324 6789
www.shigerubanarchitects.com

MASAKI ENDOH
EDH ENDOH DESIGN HOUSE
#101, 2-13-8, Honmachi,
Shibuya-ku, Tokyo 151-0071
PHONE: +81 3 3377 6293
FAX: +81 3 3377 6293

DAIGO ISHII + FUTURE-SCAPE ARCHITECTS
Yahagi Building 401
1-19-14 Yoyogi
Shibuya-ku, Tokyo 151-0053
PHONE: +81 3 5350 0855
FAX: +81 3 5350 0854
www.future-scape.co.jp

KENGO KUMA & ASSOCIATES
2-24-8, Minami-Aoyama
Minato-ku, Tokyo 107-0062
PHONE: +81 3 3401 7721
FAX: +81 3 3401 7778
www.kkaa.co.jp

PROFESSOR YOSHIFUMI NAKAMURA
3-45-4 Okusawa, 3rd Floor
Setagaya-ku, Tokyo 158-0083
PHONE: +81 3 5754 3222
FAX: +81 3 5754 3223

EIZO SHIINA & ASSOCIATES
4-6-7 Seijo
Setagaya-ku, Tokyo 157-0066
PHONE: +81 3 3482 8333
FAX: +81 3 3482 7333
www.e-shiina.com

DESIGN

YUKIKO HANAI
Engyo Bld. 7th Floor
7-15-14 Roppongi
Minato-Ku, Tokyo 106-0032
PHONE: +81 3 3404 1876
FAX: +81 3 3405 1047
www.hanai.co.jp

RIEKO KAWABE
Nippon ya kobo
2-4-6-102 Mita
Minato-ku, Tokyo 106-0032
PHONE: +81 3 3452 3111
FAX: +81 3 3452 1146
www.miyabigoto.com

ANTIQUES

YOSHIHIRO TAKISHITA
YOSHIHIRO TAKISHITA HOUSE
5-15-5 Kajiwara
Kamakura-shi 247-0063
PHONE: +81 467 43 1496
FAX: +81 467 43 7338
www.nokosokai.org

RYOKANS

THE TAWARAYA RYOKAN
Fuyacho Anekoji-agaru
Nakagyo-ku, Kyoto 604-8094
PHONE: +81 75 211 5566
FAX: +81 75 211 2204

YOSHIDA SANSO
59-1 Yoshida
Shimooji-cho
Sakyo-ku, Kyoto 606-8314
PHONE: +81 75 771 6125
FAX: +81 75 771 5667
www.yoshidasanso.com

HOSHI ONSEN – CHOJUKAN
650 Nagai
Niiharu-mura
Tone-gun, Gunma-ken 379-1401
PHONE: +81 278 66 0005
FAX: +81 278 66 0003

HOUSES TO RENT

DREAM HOUSE
Contact: Tourist Office Matsunoyama
1212-2 Matsunoyama
Tokamachi-shi, Niigata-ken 942-1492
PHONE: +81 25 596 3134
FAX: +81 25 596 2255
www.matsunoyama.com/dream

HOUSE OF LIGHT
Contact: Accommodation Service
2891 Ueno-Ko
Tokamachi-shi, Niigata-ken 948-0122
PHONE: +81 25 761 1090

IORI NISHIROKKAKU-CHO
105-1 Nishirokkaku-cho
Shinmachi Nishi-iru
Rokkaku-dori
Nagakyo-ku, Kyoto 604-8212
PHONE: +81 75 352 0211
www.kyoto-machiya.com

IORI NISHIOSHIKOJI-CHO
119 Nishioshikoji-cho
Higashinotoin Nishi-iru
Oshikoji-dori
Nagakyo-ku, Kyoto 604-0842
PHONE: +81 75 352 0211
www.kyoto-machiya.com

VISITING

GO'O SHRINE
Gotanji
Naoshima, Kagawa 761-3110
PHONE: +81 87 892 2030
www.naoshima-is.co.jp

SUGIMOTO HOUSE
Contact: Foundation Naraya-Sugimoto Residence
116 Yada-machi
Ayanokoji Nishi-iru
Shimogyo-ku, Kyoto 600-8442
www.sugimotoke.jp

OTHER ENTRIES

Alex Kerr
c/o Iori Corporation
144-6, Sujiya-cho, Takatsuji-agaru
Tominokoji
Shimogyo-ku, Kyoto 600-8061
PHONE: +81 75 352 0211
E-MAIL: info@kyoto-machiya.com
www.alex-kerr.com

Masatoshi Izumi
c/o The Isamu Noguchi Garden Museum Japan
3519 Mure, Mure-cho
Kita-gun, Kagawa 761-0121
PHONE: +81 87 870 1500
FAX: +81 87 845 0505

© 2006 TASCHEN GmbH
Hohenzollernring 53, D–50672 Köln
www.taschen.com

To stay informed about forthcoming TASCHEN titles,
please request our magazine at www.taschen.com/
magazine or write to TASCHEN, Hohenzollernring 53,
D-50672 Cologne, Germany, contact@taschen.com,
Fax: +49-221-254919. We will be happy to send you
a free copy of our magazine which is filled with
information about all of our books.

Concept, editing and layout by
Angelika Taschen, Cologne
Design by dieSachbearbeiter, Berlin
General Project Management by
Stephanie Bischoff, Cologne
Lithography by Thomas Grell, Cologne
French translation by Philippe Safavi, Paris
German translation by Christiane Burkhardt, Munich

Printed in Italy

ISBN-10: 3-8228-4594-9
ISBN-13: 978-3-8228-4594-3
(Edition with English/German cover)

ISBN-10: 3-8228-4596-5
ISBN-13: 978-3-8228-4596-7
(Edition with French cover)

TASCHEN'S
LIFESTYLE SERIES
Edited by Angelika Taschen

"Tropical elegance: what sets almost all the villas and lodges presented
in this volume apart is the naturalness with which inside
and out, living space and luxuriant nature in Bali intermingle."
Vogue, Munich on *Living in Bali*

IN PREPARATION:
The Hotel Book
Great Escapes Central
America

The Hotel Book
Great Escapes City

  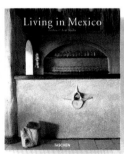 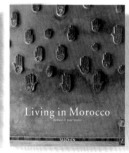 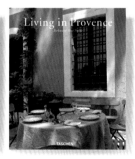

IN PREPARATION:
Inside Italy
Inside Spain
Living in Barcelona
Living in Rome